American Architecture Comes of Age

The MIT Press
Cambridge, Massachusetts,
and London, England

American Architecture Comes of Age

European Reaction to H. H. Richardson and Louis Sullivan

Leonard K. Eaton

This book was designed by the MIT Press Design Department.

It was set in Alphatype Alpha Gothic by University Graphics, Inc.,
printed on Oxford Sheerwhite Opaque
by Halliday Lithograph Corp.,
and bound by Halliday Lithograph Corp.
in the United States of America.

A list of photographic credits begins on p. 243.

Library of Congress Cataloging in Publication Data
Eaton, Leonard K
    American architecture comes of age.
    Bibliography: p.
    1. Architecture—U.S. 2. Architecture, Modern—
19th century—U.S. 3. Richardson, Henry Hobson, 1838–
1886. 4. Sullivan, Louis Henri, 1856–1924. I. Title.
NA710.E24   720'.973   76–171556
ISBN 0–262–05010–2

For Mary and Loring Staples

The theme of this book is the maturity of American architecture as an episode in the continuing cultural dialogue between Europe and America. The chief actors in the story are
the European architects who responded to the ideas and
designs of H. H. Richardson and Louis Sullivan in the 1890s
and in the first decade of this century. By their reaction to
these two major figures, the Europeans showed that American architecture had come of age. It is necessary to stress
this point, since Frank Lloyd Wright has been viewed for so
many years as the first American architect to exert any real
international influence. The impact of the great publication
of Wright's work by the Wasmuth Verlag of Berlin in 1910
is well known. Mies van der Rohe touched upon it in his
eloquent tribute to Wright written for the exhibition at the
Museum of Modern Art in 1941, and several art historians
have discussed the problem, notably Vincent Scully in his
fine article, "Frank Lloyd Wright versus the International
Style," *Art News* of March 1954, pp. 32–35 and 64–66. In
this book there is very little about the influence of Wright.
It deals with a different problem altogether.

A word is in order on the focus and form of this work. I
offer to the reader a series of essays on the significance of
American architecture in the British Isles, Scandinavia, the
Netherlands, and the German-speaking lands at the turn of
the century. The selection was made not from any deep
preference for these nations but because they happen to be
the places where American architecture was important in
the period under discussion. My failure to include material
from France, Spain, and Italy requires an explanation.

The omission of France from the list is particularly striking.
France was, of course, this country's first ally, and its cultural impact during the Revolutionary era was substantial.
Major L'Enfant provided the basic plan for the new city of
Washington, Pierre Mangin designed the New York City Hall,
and Thomas Jefferson certainly incorporated elements of
a French *maison de plaisance* into his beloved house at

Monticello. In the middle decades of the nineteenth century Richard M. Hunt and H. H. Richardson began the tradition of American architectural students at the Ecole des Beaux-Arts; both later operated their offices on the model of a French teaching atelier. After 1880 the French were extremely well informed about American developments in architecture. French architectural journals contained many articles on American building techniques, and French observers of the American scene were exceedingly perceptive. The novelist Paul Bourget wrote one of the best evaluations of the early Chicago skyscrapers, while the art dealer and critic Samuel Bing wrote a remarkable report on American achievement in the visual arts in his *La Culture artistique en Amérique* (Paris, 1895). Why, then, are there no French buildings with an American flavor in the *belle époque?*

The answer appears to be in the extraordinary strength of the French classical tradition. The late nineteenth century was an innovative period in architecture, and the two leading French innovators, Auguste Perret and Tony Garnier, thought of themselves to a remarkable extent as reinterpreting this tradition in a new material: reinforced concrete. Peter Collins has brilliantly shown that Perret was, in effect, bringing the doctrine of Blondel up to date. His greatest buildings of the pre–World War I period, notably the apartments on the Rue Franklin (1902) and the garage on the Rue Ponthieu (1904), are remarkable demonstrations of the possibilities still inherent in the tradition. A personal inspection of Garnier's buildings in Lyon has convinced me that his case was parallel to that of Perret. The buildings for the Abattoir des Mouches are surprisingly classical in feeling. For these men, both French to the core, there was simply no question of any reaction to the American achievement. It is unlikely that either of them was aware of Richardson and Sullivan.

Spain, too, was outside the sphere of influence of the American masters. To a considerable extent the architectural vitality of the Iberian Peninsula in the late nineteenth century

was concentrated in Barcelona, and in this city the movement known as *modernismo* was dominant. Its leading figure
was that remarkable architect Antonio Gaudí, who was sur-
rounded by men only slightly less gifted than himself, notably Domenech y Montaner and Pujol. These architects
were very little indebted to the classical tradition but drew on
a large variety of other sources. Gaudí thought of himself
as reestablishing the structural ideas of the Gothic age, while
certain others were closer to the Art Nouveau manner. In
much of their work one finds a definite Moorish flavor; in
no case is it American in feeling. Again, they were aware of
American work through the columns of *Rivista de la arquitectura* and *Arquitectura y construccion* but simply did not
respond to it. While Ferdinand Boberg's extremely Richardsonian fire station at Gavle, Sweden, was published in
Arquitectura y construccion (October 23, 1899) with favorable comment, one searches in vain for buildings that might
have been influenced by it.

The situation in Italy was analogous to that in Spain.
Architectural vitality was concentrated in Milan rather than
Rome, and the Lombard city witnessed the development of
the *stile floreale,* an Italian version of the Art Nouveau.
Carroll Meeks has shown that one or two of the Milanese
architects were at least aware of Wright's Prairie Houses,
and they might quite possibly have been familiar with earlier
American work. The weight of tradition, however, was so
overwhelming that Italian architects of the nineteenth century seem to have felt that their major task was to design
buildings that would harmonize with the existing urban
environment. It is not surprising that no one has yet found
any buildings of the late nineteenth century in Italy that
derive from Richardson and Sullivan.

In writing this book I have been greatly aided by many
persons and institutions in North America and Western
Europe, and it is a pleasure to acknowledge their assistance
here. My first obligation is to the late William Gray Purcell,

who, on a sunny afternoon in September 1954 told me of his meeting with Hendrik Berlage in 1906. In subsequent correspondence Mr. Purcell supplied many details of Berlage's historic American journey in 1911. Purcell's account stimulated my interest in the problem, and I incorporated much of his story in an article written for the Louis Sullivan Centennial in 1956. It was entitled "Louis Sullivan and Hendrik Berlage," and it appeared in the November 1956 issue of *Progressive Architecture.* Another article, "Richardson and Sullivan in Scandinavia," was published in the April 1964 issue of the same journal. Both pieces are presented in this volume in revised form. I am, of course, grateful to the editors of *Progressive Architecture,* Jan Rowan and the late Charles Magruder, for their sympathetic interest in my enterprises.

Numerous scholars have aided me at various stages of this work. At the University of Michigan my colleagues David Huntington, Marvin Felheim, and Lyall Powers have been extremely helpful. Professor Colin Rowe of Cornell University first called my attention to the connection between McKim, Mead & White and the Liverpool School of Architecture, and David Walker showed me the Glasgow buildings of Sir John James Burnet. Bjorn Linn helped me enormously with the Scandinavian side of the problem, as did the late Kay Fisker. Mrs. Marika Smeds was kind enough to share with me her knowledge of the Richardsonian phase in the work of Eliel Saarinen. In the Netherlands H. L. C. Jaffé and Rudolph Oxenaar were of great assistance, and in Switzerland Firman Burke and Renée Furor of the Eidgenossische Technische Hochschule pointed out to me the provocative early buildings of Karl Moser. In Vienna I benefited by consultation with Dr. Otto Graf of the Museum of the Twentieth Century, Frau Doktor Herzmansky of the Albertina, and Fräulein Vera Behalova, who is writing on the work of Adolf Loos in Prague. Among my North American colleagues I would particularly like to mention Professors Wayne Andrews of Wayne State University, Alan Gowans of the University of Victoria, and Dudley Lewis of the College of Wooster. The first two read the manuscript and gave me much valuable criticism. The unpublished Ph.D. thesis of Professor Lewis on *Evaluation of American Architecture by European Critics 1875–1900* was of inestimable value. Throughout the entire project I have been encouraged by two elder statesmen of the art historical world, Professors Nikolaus Pevsner and Henry-Russell Hitchcock. Like most of my contemporaries, I owe these gentlemen more than I can ever possibly repay.

A work of this kind is impossible without the cooperation of numerous librarians. Among those who have been especially kind are the librarians of the Royal Institute of British Architects in London, the Royal Academy of Fine Arts in Copenhagen, the Museum of Finnish Architecture in Helsinki, the Eidgenossische Technische Hochschule in Zurich, the Museum für Angewandte Kunst in Vienna, and the College of Architecture in Barcelona. At the University of Michigan William Morgan, librarian of the College of Architecture and Design, was of tremendous assistance, and at Columbia University Adolf Placzek, the Avery Librarian, was likewise extremely cooperative. Mrs. Marion Marzolf did my translations from the Scandinavian languages. To all these ladies and gentlemen go my hearty thanks.

I am also happy to acknowledge grants from the Horace H. Rackham Graduate School of the University of Michigan and the American Philosophical Society. Publication was assisted by a grant from the Graduate School. In addition, the enlightened officials of these institutions made funds available not only for travel but also, what is much more important in these days, for reflection and writing. To them I am especially grateful.

Finally, I would like to remark that this book is not intended to be the last word on the subject. The field is a rich one, the work has been rewarding, and my hope is that other investigators will join me.

American
Architecture
Comes of
Age

This volume deals with one aspect of the emergence of a distinctively American architecture in the late nineteenth century: its international impact. It is, in a sense, a contribution to the geography of art rather than to its history. One important feature of the problem is, of course, that political independence and cultural maturity are two very different ideas. After a long and bloody struggle the thirteen American colonies of Great Britain achieved their political independence from the mother country with the signing of the Treaty of Paris in 1783. During the next few decades the statesmen and intellectuals of the new republic repeatedly stressed the need for a distinctively *American* art and literature on this side of the Atlantic. None was more articulate than Thomas Jefferson in this regard, and none took a livelier personal interest in the problem. His architecture, however, demonstrates a substantial adherence to European models. Monticello, as everyone knows, is in part an American version of a Palladian country house, and it certainly shows strong French overtones. His excellent open rows of faculty housing and classrooms at the University of Virginia were punctuated with Roman temple fronts, and the library (the suggestion of Benjamin Latrobe) copied the Roman Pantheon in its general form. This is by no means remarkable. A wave of classicism was sweeping over the entire Western world in Jefferson's day, and he was simply being up-to-date, as were Schinkel in Berlin and Engel in Helsinki.[1]

There are, of course, various ways of defining the concept of cultural maturity. Recognition of achievement is one thing. Actual influence is quite another. Within a few years of the publication of a selection of his poems edited by William Rossetti in 1868, Walt Whitman had an impressive following in the British Isles. Algernon Swinburne, Edmund Gosse, George Saintsbury, Robert Louis Stevenson, and even Lord Tennyson were among his supporters. His actual influence on English literature was, however, negligible. Edgar Allan Poe, on the other hand, was not only immediately recognized by the French as an important poet but also exerted a substantial influence on the development of French symbolism. In 1852 and 1856 Charles Baudelaire wrote essays in praise of Poe and in 1857 published a volume of translations of his poetry. According to Eric Carlson, Poe was for Baudelaire a superb example of the *"poète maudit,"* a symbol of the alienated artist in frustrated rebellion against a materialistic society. Furthermore, Poe shared Baudelaire's skepticism of democracy as a social philosophy and of the doctrine of inevitable progress. Poe's theory of the close relationship of poetry and music likewise struck a responsive chord in Baudelaire, and he ultimately had a profound effect upon the whole French symbolist school of poetry. In 1876 Stéphane Mallarmé composed a moving tribute to the American writer in his famous sonnet "Le Tombeau d'Edgar Poe." Obviously the French response to Poe was very different from the English response to Whitman. It is with this creative type of interaction that we shall be concerned.[2]

The central figures of this book are the European architects who responded to H. H. Richardson and Louis Sullivan, and it is appropriate to note here that in arguing the case for the international significance of the two American designers I am proposing a revision in the architectural history of the late nineteenth century. As long ago as 1945, in the "American Postscript" to his *Outline of European Architecture,* Nikolaus Pevsner contended that Richardson was the first American architect to attain an independent national expression. He added, incorrectly, I think, that Richardson did not have much international influence. It should be noted that in pointing to the importance of Richardson, Pevsner was moving away from the traditional interpretation, which up to that time had held that the first American architect of international stature was Frank Lloyd Wright. The sumptuous publication of Wright's work in 1910 by the Berlin firm of Wasmuth Verlag established his international significance beyond question, and numerous later critics took the position that he was the only American architect ever to affect European development in any substantial way. The present writer can, in fact, clearly recall hearing this interpretation put forward in an undergraduate course in art history in 1941–1942.

The key questions, then, revolve around American relations with the Old World. At what point did American cultural expression become so strong that European artists were actually affected by it in their own work? The answer to this query will vary according to what art form one is discussing. In literature maturity was obviously gained earlier than in architecture, sculpture, or painting. Historians are now agreed that the crucial decades for the emergence of our literature are the 1840s and the 1850s. These years witnessed the appearance of major works by Poe, Emerson, Thoreau, Melville, Whitman, and Hawthorne. In 1926 Lewis Mumford called the period that produced this literature "The Golden Day," and scholars have been commenting upon it ever since. Whatever else it was, by the time of the Civil War American literature could no longer be called imitative and provincial. The poetry of Whitman and Poe, the novels of Hawthorne and Melville, and the essays of Emerson and Thoreau all exhibited a new and striking individuality. In general the forms were new and the content was new, and Europeans very quickly recognized the nature of the achievement. While no extended treatment of literature and painting is possible here, it will be useful to sketch European reactions to American work in these fields. Architecture will thus be placed in a historical context.[3]

The significance of the pre–Civil War flowering was not, of course, grasped everywhere with equal clarity. As we have indicated, Whitman had many important supporters on the English literary scene, but little actual influence. Melville, on the other hand, was generally ignored abroad, as he was in the United States after the appearance of *Moby Dick,* a book which was simply too far in advance of its time to be appreciated anywhere in the Western world when it was published

(1851). Similarly Thoreau and Hawthorne have had to wait until the twentieth century for their proper evaluations in Europe as in the United States.

As we review the impact of this group of writers on the European continent, its most striking feature is the really overwhelming reception of Whitman. Here again the French led the way. By the early 1870s he was the center of a literary controversy in Paris, and in the next decade some excellent translations began to appear. In 1886 Jules Laforgue published selections from "the astonishing American poet Walt Whitman," and both Stuart Merrill and Francis Vielé-Griffin were indebted to him. Even more important was Whitman's impact on the young André Gide in 1893. At this time, says Gay Wilson Allen, " . . . Gide was struggling to emancipate himself from two great handicaps, puritanism and the sort of physical anomalie [*sic*] which Whitman expressed in *Pent-up Aching Rivers* and other poems in *Calamus* and *Children of Adam.*"[4] For Gide, reading Whitman was a religious experience, which turned him away from his earlier Christian conception of the duality of human passion. He was reborn to both life and art. Aside from his importance to the figures who have been mentioned, Whitman entered into French literary life in many other ways. The literature on him is truly extraordinary.

The influence of Whitman in Germany came somewhat later but is equally impressive. Ferdinand Freiligrath, a political exile in England, read the Rossetti edition of Whitman's poems in 1868 and published an appreciative account of it in a German newspaper. The first few translations, however, were clumsy, and for the next two decades the poet was generally ignored. In 1889 an edition of *Leaves of Grass* came out in Switzerland, and for the first time German readers had a chance to become acquainted with such long characteristic poems as "Song of Myself" and "Out of the Cradle Endlessly Rocking." (This was probably the edition that Adolf Loos knew.) For the next two decades or so there was a real cult of Whitman in Germany, especially among younger writers such as Johannes Schlaf. Nonetheless, no really good translations of Whitman existed until 1919 when the Munich poet Hans Reisiger undertook the job. His translation, which was expanded to two volumes with a superb introduction in 1922, is considered a classic. Thomas Mann thought it was "a holy gift" to the German people. Whitman understandably fell into disfavor during the Nazi regime, but there is now apparently a new wave of interest. The Reisiger translation was reissued in 1946, and Professor Hermann Pongs has recently published a provocative analysis of Whitman and Stefan George.

Although this survey must necessarily be cursory, a word is in order on Whitman's reception in Russia. Here opinions of the American poet were at first decidedly mixed. Ivan Turgenev thought well of him, but Leo Tolstoi's attitude was ambivalent. In 1889 he received a gift copy of *Leaves of Grass* and wrote in his diary: "Received book: Whitman—ugly verses." Later he changed his view and suggested to the translator Leo Nikiforov that he undertake a Russian version of the American poet. Whitman's real impact in Russia came only in the second decade of the twentieth century, a turbulent time of war and revolution. In these years he made an enormous appeal to the artists and writers of the emerging Soviet regime. Stephen Stepanchev has commented on his astonishing impact on Russian culture during the past fifty years, observing that he has had a seminal influence on at least three generations of poets. Rightly or wrongly, the Russians have seen a correspondence between his thought and their own revolutionary ethos. Today he is as much a Russian as an American writer.[5]

In short, the reception of a foreign writer, painter, or architect depends on a number of factors that may be quite irrelevant to the intrinsic merit of his work. For a writer the availability of a good translation is perhaps most important. For an architect the quality of the reproductions of his buildings is extremely significant. Painters and sculptors are more fortunate, since the objects that they produce are portable and can be easily exhibited. Equally important in all the arts is the readiness of the culture to receive the message of the artist, as in the case of Whitman and the Russians and Poe and the French symbolists. In the late nineteenth century European architecture was ready for the message of Richardson and Sullivan. In this connection it is appropriate to observe that Richardson, like Poe, achieved his international impact without any particular effort on his part. In his maturity he made only one trip abroad (1882), and he apparently took no pains to publicize himself. One of the least verbal of architects, he never bothered to explain what he was doing, and paid no particular attention to publications of his work. These were, for the time, quite extensive. One is tempted to believe that at least a few copies of Mrs. Van Rensselaer's handsome monograph of 1888 must have crossed the Atlantic, but since the printing was only five hundred copies, it is more probable that the German publications of Graef and Hinckeldeyn played the crucial role. Wright, by way of contrast, went to Berlin to supervise a comprehensive publication of his work.

By 1890 American cultural maturity had advanced sufficiently for several important American writers to be significant on the European literary scene. For a variety of reasons Europe became attractive to American writers as a permanent residence, and the phenomenon of the expatriate writer developed. Prior to the Civil War many American writers had passed prolonged periods in Europe—one thinks immediately of Irving, Hawthorne, Howells, and Motley, all in the diplomatic service—but none had attempted to become a part of the European literary world. The central figure in this new generation was undoubtedly Henry James (1843–1916). As a young man James spent several years in Paris in the 1870s and came to know the leading figures in the French literary establishment well. He was acquainted with Flaubert, the Goncourt brothers, and Turgenev, who, like many Russian writers, thought of France as his spiritual home. This literary apprenticeship produced strong French elements in James's own work. In 1880, however, he moved permanently to England, settling first in London and finally at Lamb House, Rye. In England James was very much a part of the great literary world of his day. He knew almost all of its major figures, and was especially close to Joseph Conrad, Ford Madox Ford, and, curiously, H. G. Wells. Though none of these writers was much affected by the Jamesian style, all responded to his emphasis on psychological analysis and his development of the interior monologue, especially in his later novels. R. P. Blackmur has noted that Conrad and Ford frankly used his method, Conrad in *Chance* and *Under Western Eyes* and Ford in *The Good Soldier* and *Parade's End,* his remarkable tetralogy on World War I.[6] In Henry James America produced a writer who powerfully affected the entire course of modern fiction.

James, of course, was not the only American writer to arouse intense interest among Europeans in these years. Mark Twain was of such great interest to the English that Oxford conferred an honorary degree upon him in 1910, the first to be awarded to an American writer. Twain, however, was regarded as so American that he was inimitable. Edith Wharton was a personality in many ways more congenial to Euopean literary sensibility. She was as much a part of the Paris literary scene as James was in London. She counted the French novelist Paul Bourget among her close friends and knew the salons of the French capital well. She even wrote the first version of *Ethan Frome* in French, and her novels enjoyed a considerable popularity in translation. Numerous minor figures, such as Harold Frederic, for many years the London correspondent of *The New York Times,* might also be mentioned. Nonetheless it was James who had much the greatest impact on Europe.

In painting the story is very different. Books are, after all, portable objects, and the craft of writing can presumably be learned in one's own study. Thoreau remarked that he had traveled much in Concord. European studios with their highly developed painting techniques, and European galleries with their overwhelming supplies of the works of the old masters were irresistible magnets to young American artists all through the nineteenth century. During the early years of the republic, Gilbert Stuart, Washington Allston, and Samuel F. B. Morse continued the colonial tradition of study in London. By the middle of the century the stream of painters had shifted to Düsseldorf and in the 1870s and 1880s to Munich. Albert Bierstadt and Eastman Johnson were trained in the Rhenish city, Frank Duveneck and William Merritt Chase in the Bavarian capital. After the Civil War Paris began to emerge as an even greater center of attraction. Thomas Eakins (1844–1916) studied with Gérôme and John Singer Sargent (1856–1925) with Carolus Duran. Of course many painters, notably those of the Hudson River School, stayed at home and learned from each other or from engravings and paintings by European artists. Sometimes these generally homebred artists were able to travel abroad.

Today nineteenth-century American painting is being reevaluated, and much of it appears far more significant than it did only a few years ago. There is a new interest in the work of men like Thomas Cole, Frederic Church, and John F. Kensett, yet it would be hard to argue that any of these artists strongly affected the major currents in European painting, as James did in literature. There is good evidence that Allston had an effect on German painting, but this was a minor episode. The great movements of nineteenth-century European painting—romanticism, realism, and impressionism—developed without any particular reference to American art. In vain does one search the careers of Delacroix, Courbet, and Renoir for contacts with their American contemporaries. Often there are parallels, as in the early work of Homer, which can easily be called impressionist, and sometimes there are American versions of European styles, as in the impressionism of Weir and Twachtman and the cubism of Alfred Maurer. Though Whistler, like Poe, had an effect upon French literature (he, too, was greatly admired by Mallarmé and Baudelaire), the historian of American painting cannot note any substantial influence on European development. On the contrary, the flow of ideas has been all the other way. Charles Demuth wrote, "John Marin and I drew our inspiration from the same source, French Modernism. He brought his up in buckets. I dipped mine out with a teaspoon, but I never spilled a drop."[7]

The men who did for American painting what Poe and James had done in literature were the abstract expressionists, who burst upon the art world during the Second World War. The art historian John McCoubrey has written that the brilliant canvases of these painters have been shown and imitated from Tokyo to Paris. It is perfectly true, he notes, that their work would have been impossible without the cubist revolution and Picasso, without German expressionism and without the "accidents" of the Dada painters and the automatism of the surrealists. Still, this art is distinctively American, and very much a part of the national tradition.[8] The pictures of Jackson Pollock, Franz Kline, and Willem de Kooning for the first time made American art a world force. Of what did their contribution consist?

Although we are still so close to the events of the 1940s that a number of questions remain to be cleared up (so far there is no good book on Kline), it is clear that the crucial breakthrough was probably made by Pollock (1912–1956). The critic Sam Hunter, an acute observer of the New York scene, has commented on Pollock's " . . . willingness to expend himself extravagantly and profligately, often at the cost of the harmony and coherence of individual paintings, in order to take possession of the modern abstract picture."[9] Hunter also comments on the prodigal expenditure of psychic energy that went into Pollock's paintings and the individualism of his temperament, which links him to a whole series of American romantics from Poe to Ives and Faulkner. His art had its roots deep in his tortured subconscious, and he himself made several statements to this effect. Pollock's contemporaries exploited his breakthrough in many directions, and the entire movement had a profound effect in Europe. Perhaps the most telling testimony comes from the French painter Georges Mathieu. He played a leading role in obtaining showings for the American abstract expressionists in Paris, and wrote with bitter humor of the horror that they produced in the old guard. His own work, which the French christened *tachisme,* would have been impossible without them. With the advent of abstract expressionism, American painting came of age.[10]

In sculpture the story is parallel. Here the key figure is probably David Smith (1906–1965). He was the first American to work consistently in welded metal, beginning in 1933 after reading an article in *Cahiers d' art* on the iron constructions of Picasso and Julio Gonzalez. It took Smith some years to develop his own independent style, but by 1945 he had arrived at an expression just as forceful in sculpture as Pollock, Kline, and De Kooning in painting. He, too, exhibited around the world and was widely influential.

The first American building to have a real impact across the Atlantic was the Eastern Penitentiary in Philadelphia by John Haviland (1823–1825). Sir Charles Barry's Pentonville Prison in London of 1841–1842 closely followed its radial plan, with the doors of all cells visible from a central hall. It is doubtful, however, that this episode can be considered in our context, since Haviland was himself an English architect who had settled in Philadelphia in 1816.[11] It seems, in fact, to have been an isolated case in the pre–Civil War period. The architecture of Latrobe, Mills, and Strickland was no more influential abroad than was the painting of Cole, Church, or Kensett.

About 1875 an important change in the attitude of European architects began to occur. The primary reason for this shift was the widespread interest in the proposed Centennial Exposition at Philadelphia. In 1876 more European architects and architectural writers crossed the Atlantic than at any previous time in the nineteenth century. During the next twenty-five years coverage of American developments in the European architectural press was substantial. Between 1875 and 1900 there were more than one hundred discussions and illustrations of architecture in the United States in *The Builder* (London), at least forty-two references in *La semaine des constructeurs* (Paris), forty in *Le moniteur des architectes* (Paris), thirty-eight in *Architektonische Rundschau* (Stuttgart), and thirty-seven in the *Deutsche Bauzeitung* (Berlin). This body of material in the leading journals was supplemented by a good many articles in lesser-known periodicals in other languages. For any European architect who was curious about what was going on in the United States, the evidence was available.[12]

Interest in American architecture was not, of course, equally distributed throughout this period, nor was it confined exclusively to the architectural journals. After the spate of articles in 1876–1877 there was a falling off for a few years and then a recrudescence in 1886, which Dudley Lewis terms the pivotal year. The probable reason for this second stir of attention was, ironically enough, the untimely death of America's greatest architect, H. H. Richardson. In 1885 the *American Architect and Building News* had taken a poll of its readers to determine the ten most beautiful buildings in the United States. Richardson's Trinity Church in Boston was easily ranked first with 84 percent of the total vote. Richardson's Albany City Hall, Sever Hall at Harvard, New York State Capitol, and Town Hall at North Easton, Massachusetts, were ranked seventh, eighth, ninth, and tenth, respectively. Such a remarkable show of unanimity by the profession naturally attracted a great deal of notice, and the interest in Richardson abroad was undoubtedly increased by his death the next year. Many of the obituaries in the European press regretted that his work had not been better known during his lifetime, and in 1888 Alfred Waterhouse implied that he would have been awarded the gold medal of the Royal Institute of British Architects (R.I.B.A.) if he had lived. After 1886 coverage of American developments was more intensive, reaching a high point in 1893 when large numbers of European architects came to the United States for the World's Fair at Chicago. Finally, in the years just prior to the turn of the century, it tapered off, as European architectural writers became more concerned with the exciting new developments in their own countries.

In one sense this outpouring of critical and interpretive writing is in itself a powerful argument for the maturity of American architecture. More than one author at the end of the century remarked that two decades previously it would have been unthinkable for a European to go to the United States for study, whereas by the late 1890s, it was a perfectly reasonable thing to do. American solutions to the problems of the tall office building and the individual dwelling house were particularly admired. In terms of style, however, it was unquestionably the giant figure of H. H. Richardson, which, for Europeans, overshadowed all other Americans of the age. Indeed, so overwhelming was his impact that many European readers must have believed that he was the only American architect of true distinction.

What was the exact nature of the achievement that enabled Richardson to dominate his profession so completely? We should first observe that his social background and education fitted him ideally for a position of influence in the America of his day. He was born of the Louisiana plantation aristocracy in 1838, and like many young men of his class, was originally destined for the military academy at West Point. Fortunately for American architecture, a slight speech impediment prevented his appointment, and instead he went north to Harvard, matriculating with the class of 1859, which also included Henry Adams, a good friend and understanding critic in his later life. At some point in his Harvard career his objective changed from civil engineering to architecture, and after graduation he went to Paris to study at the world-famed Ecole des Beaux-Arts. The sources of the decision appear to lie in a determination to excel in the design of monumental public buildings, an aspect of architecture in which the French were then preeminent.

Like two of his contemporaries, Adams and William Dean Howells, Richardson spent the Civil War period in Europe, but his years abroad were not so financially carefree as theirs. In 1862 the comfortable remittances from home ceased altogether, and thereafter he supported himself by working in the office of Henri Labrouste, the great French expert on library building. This experience game him a lifelong regard for problems of planning and construction. Coupled with the traditional logic of the Ecole, it made him unquestionably the best-trained architect of his generation when he returned to the United States in 1865. It is interesting that the work of his first years of practice owed very little to Second Empire Paris. His churches were in the fashionable Gothic revival manner, and his houses were distinctly Queen Anne. For certain details he was indebted to the Englishman Richard Norman Shaw, whose work he apparently knew through magazine publication. The real and solid benefits of his French training emerged only in later years.

The turning point in Richardson's career came in the years 1870–1873 when he developed a Romanesque revival style, first in the Brattle Square Church of Boston, and then much more fully in Trinity Church in the same city. The Romanesque was the round-arched, barrel-vaulted style of the twelfth century in Western Europe, but it must be stated that in turning to it for inspiration Richardson went far beyond the traditional historicism of his day. What he was seeking was its primitive strength and vigor; the evocation of the Middle Ages was in itself of little interest to him, and his buildings were only vaguely archeological. They made an overwhelming impression on Richardson's contemporaries by the boldness of their compositions and the forcefulness of their stonework. In an age of jerry-building, Richardson not only insisted on the integrity of the masonry wall but often employed a powerful, rock-faced ashlar to obtain a characteristically strong textural effect. In a sense they were excellent symbols for his clients, who included some of the foremost industrial tycoons and political spoilsmen of the day. As Lewis Mumford has pointed out, Richardson must be seen as an architect very much in tune with his own period. He did not reject the forces of industrialism but sought to discipline them.

The Richardsonian Romanesque thus came to be an architecture broadly applicable to the problems of the new industrial era. Railroad stations, libraries, and commercial structures were all done in this manner, and his office became the prototype of the large American architectural organization. It must be stressed that while Richardson knew the historic styles perfectly, he was, after Trinity Church, hardly ever archeological. He handled the Romanesque in an almost incredibly free way, and was never concerned with the virtue of correctness. This was an enormous innovation in the nineteenth century, an era that had been plagued by the battle of the styles. In his late years he did a series of important buildings from which historicism was eliminated almost entirely. Of these the most significant was certainly the Marshall Field Wholesale Store of 1884–1886, a structure that had a profound influence upon Louis Sullivan and the Chicago School. It is, in fact, fair to say that no single architect in American history ever dominated his period as did H. H. Richardson. A whole school of followers arose, and Richardsonian buildings sprang up throughout the land. Versions of his Allegheny County Courthouse can be found in Minneapolis, Toronto, and Los Angeles. Almost single-handedly, H. H. Richardson raised American architecture from the incredibly low level to which it had sunk in the 1860s and made it once again a public art of major significance.[13]

The contribution of Louis Sullivan (1856–1924) was of a different order. Whereas Richardson was primarily a reformer, Sullivan was a programmatic innovator. Born of immigrant parents in a New England where transcendental ideas lingered on, Sullivan was a precocious youth who studied at the famous English High School of Boston and then, briefly, at the newly founded school of architecture of the Massachusetts Institute of Technology. Dissatisfied with its emphasis on the historic styles, he left after a few months to obtain practical experience, first in the office of the noted Philadelphia architect Frank Furness, and then more importantly with William Le Baron Jenney, who was probably the foremost designer of commercial structures in Chicago during the 1870s. The experience with Jenney gave Sullivan a lasting interest in engineering problems, but he felt the need for further education. He, too, attended the Ecole des Beaux-Arts, and while disliking its historicism, acquired a deep regard for the qualities of logic and discipline that it taught. Not bothering to take a diploma, he returned to Chicago and in 1879 went into partnership with Dankmar Adler, a gifted structural engineer who needed an architectural designer. For the next fifteen years the firm of Adler and Sullivan was immensely successful and became nationally known for the excellence of its commercial buildings.

During this period Sullivan was primarily concerned with the problem of the tall building and the architectural expression of the steel frame. More than any of his contemporaries Sullivan saw that the basic difficulty was to make tall buildings *look* tall and that the new forms of skeleton construction had invalidated the Renaissance approach to design that had governed architecture for centuries. (Richardson, whom Sullivan followed in his Auditorium Hotel of 1886–1889, did not live long enough to employ the new techniques.) In his best buildings of the 1890s, notably the Prudential Guaranty in Buffalo of 1895 and the Carson, Pirie, Scott Store of 1899–1901 Sullivan achieved an elegant structural expression that architects have admired ever since. In addition, he was much concerned with the function of ornament in architecture. Believing that a properly designed building should have the same organic structure as a plant, he thought of the ornament as corresponding to the flower, and often sheathed his works in marvelously detailed terra-cotta, sometimes with a foliate motif. Not surprisingly, he was a convinced Darwinian and an excellent amateur naturalist. Much of the organic theory of architecture, which is usually associated with his greatest pupil, Frank Lloyd Wright, can be traced to the ornament of Louis Sullivan. Wright, who was in Sullivan's office for almost five years, always acknowledged his debt to his "lieber meister."

In addition to the ideas of Darwin, many other strains entered into Sullivan's thinking about his art. Of an extremely theoretical and literary turn of mind, he was, in fact, the first American architect to study deeply the relation of his profession to the society of which it was a part and the first to evolve a true philosophy of architecture. His vision was essentially poetic and religious. A devoted admirer of Walt Whitman, he corresponded with the poet, and his own prose often had a distinctly Whitmanesque flavor. An important aspect of his career is that he wrote prolifically, especially after 1900, when public taste was turning away from the direction for which he stood and toward a neoclassical revivalism. The last twenty-four years of his life were, in fact, marked by public neglect, personal bitterness, and alcoholism. Through it all he stubbornly maintained his integrity. Though forsaken by the magnates of Chicago, he was able to do a series of small-town banks that rank among the masterworks of American architecture, and his memory was treasured by a few steadfast disciples, especially Wright. Hence later generations of architects have tended to see him as a tragic figure and a prophet. There is a certain fine irony in the posthumous award of the gold medal of the American Institute of Architects to Louis Henri Sullivan in 1952.[14]

While Sullivan had his followers in Europe, as did the academic firm of McKim, Mead & White, it was chiefly Richardson who was emulated by the generation of architects who came to the fore in the British Isles and on the Continent in the 1890s. He is therefore, like Poe and Whitman earlier, and Pollock and David Smith later, a central figure in the development of American culture. Like a pioneer, he led the way. Hence much of this study deals with what Richardson meant to men like Adolf Loos in Austria, Ferdinand Boberg in Sweden, and Eliel Saarinen in Finland. These were all men who played important roles in the vital development of European architecture prior to World War I. That they turned to Richardson and Sullivan for inspiration seems sufficient proof that American architecture had come of age in a broad cultural sense by the decade of the nineties. It was no longer provincial, as it had been up to this time.

In the field of architecture the United States had ceased to be a colony and had become an important part of Atlantic civilization.

Notes

1. In my interpretation I find myself somewhat at odds with the brilliant study of Professor William Pierson, *American Buildings and Their Architects: The Colonial and Neo-Classical Styles* (New York, 1970). Robert Mills was, as Pierson shows, an exceptionally capable architect, but I am unable to see that his treasury building of 1836–1842 is essentially different from the contemporary work of Schinkel and Engel. I cannot agree that it was an announcement of cultural independence.

2. On Whitman see the section on "Walt Whitman and World Literature" in Gay Wilson Allen, *Walt Whitman Handbook* (Chicago, 1946); on Poe in France see *The Recognition of Edgar Allan Poe,* ed. Eric Carlson (Ann Arbor, 1966), p. 3.

3. Professor Marvin Felheim of the University of Michigan has pointed out to me that it was, ironically enough, Cooper and Irving who made Europe conscious of American literature. These two authors can, however, be understood as essentially British writers (in

the manner of Scott and Goldsmith) who simply happened to be born in the United States. Their appeal was not on the basis of any strong American quality. They appeared as English writers who had simply used American settings. Cooper also foreshadowed James in his extended European sojourn (1826–1833).

4. Allen, *Whitman Handbook,* p. 500.

5. On Whitman in Germany and Russia see the selected essays in *Walt Whitman Abroad,* ed. Gay Wilson Allen (Syracuse, 1955).

6. R. P. Blackmur makes this observation in his chapter on James in vol. 2 of *Literary History of the United States,* ed. Robert E. Spiller, Willard Thorp, Thomas H. Johnson, and Henry S. Canby, (New York, 1948), p. 1043.

7. Quoted in Sam Hunter, *Modern American Painting and Sculpture* (New York, 1959), p. 80.

8. John W. McCoubrey, *The American Tradition in Painting* (New York, 1963), p. 8.

9. Hunter, *Modern American Painting and Sculpture,* p. 131.

10. Georges Mathieu, *Au-delà du tachisme* (Paris, 1963). See especially pp. 58–70, "La première confrontation avec la peinture américaine."

11. Henry-Russell Hitchcock, *Early Victorian Architecture in Britain* (New Haven, 1954), p. 191.

12. Here, and elsewhere in this book, I am heavily indebted to the Ph.D. thesis of Dudley A. Lewis (University of Wisconsin, 1962). It is entitled "Evaluations of American Architecture by European Critics, 1875–1900."

13. The key works for the interpretation of H. H. Richardson are Mrs. Schuyler Van Rensselaer, *Henry Hobson Richardson and His Works* (Boston, 1888; also available in a reprint edition, Park Forest, Ill., 1967) and Henry-Russell Hitchcock, *The Architecture of H. H. Richardson and His Times,* revised ed. (Cambridge, Mass., 1966). Mention should also be made of the excellent essay by Lewis Mumford in *The South in Architecture* (New York, 1941).

14. In the Sullivan bibliography the most important single item is still Hugh Morrison, *Louis Sullivan: Prophet of Modern Architecture* (New York, 1935). It may be supplemented by the superb pictorial essay of John Szarkowski, *The Idea of Louis Sullivan* (Minneapolis, 1956) and Sullivan's own *Autobiography of an Idea* (New York, 1924; reprint edition, New York, 1956).

For British architects, American developments in the late nineteenth century were a matter of great interest. Dudley Lewis has pointed out that they become increasingly curious about them after 1882.[1] In that year Arthur John Gale, the first winner of the Godwin Bursary, used it for study in the United States. On his return to England, Gale lectured twice before the R.I.B.A., paying particular attention to structural systems and mechanical equipment. He also remarked that the tastelessness that had characterized American architectural design was no longer so conspicuous as it had once been. On the whole English architects seem to have thought that American architects were progressive in building technology but backward in architectural design. This attitude changed with their recognition of the overwhelming importance of H. H. Richardson, who himself paid a visit to London in 1882. During the short span of years remaining before Richardson's death in 1886, at least two prominent Englishmen called on him at his home in Brookline, Massachusetts. One of these was the architectural critic and writer Horace Townsend, who, in 1894, published an article on his visit in *The Magazine of Art,* illustrating it with photographs and sketches of the architect's work. Townsend's remarks demonstrate that he not only visited the large number of Richardson's buildings in the Boston area but also traveled west to Cincinnati and Chicago to see the imposing structures that Richardson was building in those cities. He concludes his account with a reference to the home of the painter Hubert von Herkomer as "the only work on this side of the Atlantic by which the genius of the architect may to some extent be judged"[2] (Figure 2).

Herkomer was the other visitor from England, and his meeting with Richardson occurred in 1886. A skilled portraitist and a Royal Academician, he did a portrait of Richardson in return for a design of a country house which he planned to build at Bushey in Hertfordshire. The house was actually constructed in 1889–1890, and Herkomer and his

Figure 1
Sir John and Lady Jean
Burnet at Killermont,
Farnham, 1930

Figure 2
H. H. Richardson,
"Lululand," Gateway,
Bushey, Hertfordshire,
1889–1890

family occupied it in 1894. Henry-Russell Hitchcock indicates that "the executed detail was largely redesigned by
Herkomer"[3] and that little of Richardson's basic conception
remains. The structure was named "Lululand" after Herkomer's first wife. Nikolaus Pevsner has written, "Of Sir
Hubert von Herkomer's, the celebrated portrait painter's
house, only the entrance survives. It must at all costs be preserved, as it is the only European work of the best American
later nineteenth-century architect, H. H. Richardson."[4]
Robert Koch has noted that Herkomer's school at Bushey
was a popular meeting place for progressively minded young
English artists during the nineties and that they must have
thought of his house as "a symbol of unconventional originality."[5]

Knowledge of Richardson in England was disseminated
through a variety of sources other than Lululand. From 1877
onward, his work was widely published in professional journals, and it evidently attracted a substantial audience. As we
have noted previously, Richardson was an Honorary Corresponding Member of the Royal Institute of British Architects, and Alfred Waterhouse implied in his obituary for the
R.I.B.A. *Journal of Proceedings* that he would have been
nominated for the Royal Gold Medal if he had lived longer.
Some of Waterhouse's own work, notably the King's Weigh
House Church in Mayfair (1885, Figure 3), has a curiously
Richardsonian flavor, but the massing, polychromy, and fenestration are entirely different from those of the American
master.

The leading Richardsonian architect in England was the arts
and crafts designer, Charles Harrison Townsend (1852–
1928). Like his contemporary, Charles F. Annesley Voysey,
Townsend was experienced in the design of wallpapers and
textiles, and like Lethaby and Ashbee he was very much a
public personality. He lectured widely, wrote many articles
on architectural subjects, and edited Nash's *Mansions.* In
addition he was a master of the Art Workers' Guild and or-

Figure 3
Alfred Waterhouse, King's
Weigh House Church,
Mayfair, London, 1885

ganized many of its European tours. He also participated in the organization and hanging of various exhibitions of British art on the continent. As with his English contemporaries, his own work received favorable attention abroad, especially in Germany.[6]

Townsend's first truly Richardsonian building was the Bishopsgate Institute (Figure 4). This structure was opened by the prominent Tory politico Lord Roseberry on Nov. 24, 1894, and was therefore probably designed in 1893. The site on Bishopsgate Street was only twenty-four feet wide, and the program included both a meeting hall and a library (the building is sometimes known as the Bishopsgate Free Library). The section shows that Townsend provided a toplit hall that could be used for lectures and exhibitions and also a good-sized reading room. It is interesting that in England and Sweden several of the first Richardsonian buildings were libraries; European architects must have been impressed by his treatment of this building type. The major element in the red limestone facade is a powerful round arch with ornamental details of terra cotta. A German writer of 1902 noted the simplicity of its composition and the fine effect of the fenestration.[7]

Even more Richardsonian was Townsend's first project of 1896 for the Whitechapel Art Gallery (Figure 5). This structure was to provide a permanent home for exhibitions that had been held in various places in the area for seventeen years. The illustration here is of a pastel and gouache drawing shown at the Royal Academy, and it loses something in black and white. In the High Victorian tradition, Townsend thought of his building as a color study as well as from a purely architectonic point of view. He used cut stone of a warm yellow tone for his exterior walling, contrasting it effectively with the reddish yellow and white marble of the central doorway. Green slate was employed in the flanking towers. The final design (Figure 6) was equally Richardsonian but less ambitious. Instead of the five round arches at the second

Figure 4
Charles Harrison Townsend,
Bishopsgate Institute,
1893–1894

Figure 5
Charles Harrison Townsend,
First Project, Whitechapel
Art Gallery, London, 1896

Figure 6
Charles Harrison Townsend,
Final Design, Whitechapel
Art Gallery, London, 1898

Figure 7
Charles Harrison Townsend,
Horniman Free Museum,
London, 1901

level, a series of squareheaded windows was employed, and
the corner towers were reduced in size. The doorway remained a compelling feature, and in both buildings there was
a lavish decorative program in the manner of the Arts and
Crafts Movement. A contemporary writer observed that
Townsend " . . . has eschewed any positive historical style
and succeeded in being thoroughly architectural, not to say
monumental in his design."[8]

The quality of monumentality may have been what attracted
Townsend to Richardson, and it certainly received strong expression in the last of his important public buildings, the
Horniman Free Museum of 1902 (Figure 7). F. J. Horniman,
M.P., was an art collector who sometimes threw his house
open to the public. When his collection became popular, he
conceived the idea of erecting a museum and presenting it to
the city. It is today an important center for the study of William Morris. The site presented substantial difficulties. It
was narrow and steep, so Townsend split the building into
two parts of about equal size. The ground was clayey, and
great precautions had to be taken before the foundation
stone of the tower could be laid. The walling material was
Doulting stone, a shelly, granular limestone that is a grayish
brown in color, and as with the Whitechapel Gallery, the decorative program was lavish. The round arches of the doorways were carried through on the interior, and at the lintels
there was foliate carving that was also rather Richardsonian
in character. It was, for the time, a practical building, easy of
access, spacious, and unpretentious in internal planning. As
with the Whitechapel Gallery, *The Studio* stressed its originality: "It stands there at Forest Hill as a new series of frank
and fearless thoughts expressed and co-ordinated in stone."[9]
The language suggests some of the novelty that the British
seem to have found in Richardson.

Aside from Richardson, Great Britain also drew on two
principal American streams of architectural thought in the
late nineteenth and early twentieth century: the neoclas-

sicism of the East and the secessionism of Louis Sullivan and
the Chicago School. Indeed, the polarity between the architecture of Glasgow and that of London in these years curiously parallels the opposition between New York and Chicago.
Several of the writer's colleagues who have visited Glasgow
have commented on the similarity of the city's architectural
quality to that of Chicago, and there are many parallels between the career of Sullivan and that of Glasgow's greatest
architect, Charles Rennie Mackintosh. Both were brilliant
men with tragic personal weaknesses, and both felt compelled to stay in their cities and fight the local philistines.
After 1910 both moved increasingly away from architecture,
Sullivan into philosophy and Mackintosh into watercolor
painting. The resemblance is striking. [10]

   The port of entry for American neoclassicism was Liverpool,
where, in 1904, Sir Charles Herbert Reilly assumed the direc-
torship of the school of architecture. Reilly, who was himself
an R.I.B.A. gold medalist in 1938, was a particular admirer of
the American academic tradition. In 1932, on the occasion of
his retirement from the chair of architecture, a large volume
was published in his honor. It was entitled *The Book of the
Liverpool School of Architecture* (Liverpool and London,
1932). In an introductory essay, Stanley C. Ramsay wrote:

The reaction from the French standard to a more national
style set the pioneers adventuring in America. Liverpool, as
the chief port for Americans adventuring in this country, was
peculiarly susceptible to American influence and Reilly was,
architecturally speaking, one of the first to cross the Herring
Pond. Here again time mocks our little systems with their at-
tendant enthusiasms, and today the architecture of McKim,
Mead, and White is considered by the elect as *vieux jeu.* But
fifteen to twenty years ago I can remember the intense excite-
ment that the publication of this American work caused: it
seemed to have all the breadth of the French with the refine-
ment of the Italian, and yet somehow was wonderfully Anglo-
Saxon. Comparisons were made between the reaction of
America on this country, and the influence that the Colonial
Greek architecture exerted on Athens. [11]

   Reilly himself wrote an enthusiastic volume on *McKim,
Mead & White* (New York, 1924) in which he saw their work

as one of the great determining forces in the architecture of the period and referred to the resemblance of the work of some of the younger English architects to that of their American confreres. Late in life he recalled that his contacts with the American profession had enabled him to place annually about six fourth-year students in American offices to gain practical experience. Since these offices were generally those of the large Eastern firms which carried on the neoclassical manner, an existing direction in English architecture was noticeably strengthened. Thomas Hastings of the New York firm of Carrère & Hastings was a particularly close friend; in 1924 the two actually collaborated on the design of Devonshire House, an immense Italianate pile in Piccadilly (Figure 8). A few years later Reilly wrote an obituary notice for Hastings in the *Journal of the Royal Institute of British Architects.* The latter had meanwhile become the third American to be a gold medalist of that organization. As early as 13 March 1891, Alexander Koch, the editor of *Academy Architecture and Architectural Review,* wrote to McKim, Mead & White asking for photographs of the firm's work. He remarked, "Your firm's name has been *specially given* to me as doing the best work in the States."[12]

The effect of the close study of American neoclassicism fostered by Reilly is visible in certain buildings illustrated in the Liverpool memorial volume. One of the most knowing of his students must have been Harold A. Dod, whose Atheneum Club in Liverpool (Figure 9) bears a strong relationship to similar buildings in New York, such as the Metropolitan Club of 1894 by McKim, Mead & White (Figure 10). Another Liverpool building in the same vein was the Head Office for Martin's Bank Limited (Figure 11) of 1928 by Herbert J. Rowse, much less polished and elegant in proportion. In an era of imperial expansion Reilly's students spread his gospel all over the globe. One of the most impressive structures of its kind was the headquarters of the Egyptian Telephone and Telegraph Company in Cairo by Maurice Beresford (Figure

Figure 8
Carrère & Hastings with
Charles H. Reilly as consul-
tant, Devonshire House,
London, 1924

Figure 9
Harold A. Dod, Atheneum
Club, Liverpool, 1924–1928

Figure 10
McKim, Mead & White,
Metropolitan Club, New
York, 1894

Figure 11
Herbert J. Rowse, Head
Office for Martin's Bank
Limited, Liverpool, 1928

Figure 12
Maurice Beresford,
Egyptian Telephone and
Telegraph Company,
Cairo, Egypt, n.d.

Figure 13
Beresford House,
Johannesburg, South
Africa, 1928

Figure 14
John Burnet & Son,
Glasgow Institute of Fine
Arts, Glasgow, 1878

12); it somehow seems the very thing to overawe the fellahin. Even closer to the McKim, Mead & White manner is Beresford House in Johannesburg, South Africa of 1928 (Figure 13). The architect is unknown, but the quoining and the Bramantesque window detailing are certainly familiar to any student of the New York firm's work.

If Mackintosh was the Sullivan of Glasgow, Sir John James Burnet (1857–1938) was its D. H. Burnham. Burnet, the son of a well-known Glasgow practitioner, was first trained in his father's offices, and in 1874 went over to Paris for study in the Atelier Jean Louis Pascal, which Charles Follen McKim (1847–1909) had attended prior to the Franco-Prussian War. Having taken the Diplôme du Gouvernement in architecture and engineering in 1877, he returned to Glasgow to join his father's firm, and in 1878 was responsible for its victory in a competition for new galleries for the Glasgow Institute of Fine Arts (Figure 14). This was truly a refined and scholarly performance, undoubtedly the most polished academic building the city had seen up to that time. It was a remarkable design for a young man barely twenty-one years of age. Not surprisingly young Burnet became his father's partner shortly thereafter.

In the 1880s the firm of John Burnet & Son (after 1886, Burnet, Son, & Campbell) was responsible for a number of excellent business buildings in Glasgow, many of them in the Beaux-Arts manner. At the same time, nevertheless, we can observe a developing interest in American work, particularly in Louis Sullivan and the Chicago School. Some of this interest may have come from the increased attention paid to American architecture in British periodicals, but it was probably reinforced by a study of American magazines. Dr. Andor Gomme, coauthor of a superb book on Glasgow, declares, "The more important American journals were always taken in the best Glasgow offices."[13] The Scotch metropolis, the second city in the kingdom, was, like Chicago, fiercely independent in character, and evidently looked outward across the Atlantic in its effort to escape the hegemony of London. The first indication of America's attraction for Burnet can probably be seen in such buildings as the Atlantic Chambers of 1899 (Figures 15 and 16).

In 1896, in connection with a large hospital commission, Burnet made the first of several journeys to the United States. While his exact itinerary is not known, it seems probable that he visited both New York and Chicago. He may have met Louis Sullivan, and it is quite likely that he met McKim. At this point in his career Sullivan was still considered one of the leading designers in Chicago; he had not yet encountered the heartbreaking frustrations that were to plague him after the turn of the century, and it would have been a natural thing for Burnet to look him up. McKim, as a senior partner in the leading New York firm of his day, was an important member of the official American cultural establishment. That the two men were close friends is attested by the obituary notice for Burnet in the *Journal of the Royal Institute of British Architects,* which remarks that he had few close professional friends and that McKim was one of these.[14] Burnet himself wrote the obituary notice for McKim. It is, in fact, possible that the two were already acquainted in 1896. McKim's frequent trips to Europe, many of them in connection with the establishment of the American Academy in Rome, brought him into close contact with prominent figures in the British architectural profession. In 1903 he became the second American to receive the gold medal of the Royal Institute of British Architects (Richard Morris Hunt in 1893 was the first).

Like Burnham, Burnet was pulled in two directions. For business and industrial structures he was attracted to the line of development espoused by Sullivan and the Chicago School. The headquarters of McGeoch's hardware business of 1905 in Glasgow is perhaps the most important single example of his work in this vein (Figure 17). With its powerful unipartitite cornice and strong handling of the vertical piers,

Figure 15
Sir John James Burnet,
Atlantic Chambers,
Glasgow, 1899

Figure 16
Sir John James Burnet,
Atlantic Chambers, facade
detail, Glasgow, 1899

Figure 17
Sir John James Burnet,
McGeoch's, Glasgow, 1905

Figure 19
Sir John James Burnet,
Edward VII addition to the
British Museum, interior,
London, 1905–1914

Figure 18
Sir John James Burnet,
Edward VII addition to the
British Museum, London,
1905–1914

Figure 20
Sir John James Burnet,
Kodak Building, Kingsway,
London, 1910

it is truly an admirable building and very much in the local
tradition, which emphasizes strong modelling and plasticity
of form. While one may take exception to the sculpture over
the doorway, it is certainly one of the finest structures in the
city of Glasgow—and incidentally one of the most Sullivanian
buildings in all of Europe. For official and governmental edifices, on the other hand, it was the McKim direction that pre-
vailed. Here the great case in point is the Edward VII addition
to the British Museum, which Burnet won in a competition of
1904. This structure was one of the most important building
projects of Edwardian London, and at its completion in 1914
he received a knighthood. It is an overwhelming neoclassical
design that yet retains a curious thinness of detail quite reminiscent of McKim (Figures 18, 19). The affiliations with the
later work of D. H. Burnham & Co. are also strong, and a recent writer in the *Architectural Review* correctly observes
that "the British Museum could well be in Washington."[15]

  With the enormous success of the Edward VII galleries, commissions poured into Burnet's firm, and in 1904–1905 he
opened a London branch. By 1910 the work of this office was
his major interest, and about this time he transferred his
home to the city, although he also retained a Glasgow residence until 1914. While he did a colossal amount of work in
London, it is probable that his most important single achievement was the Kodak Building in Kingsway, designed in 1910
(Figure 20). This edifice was classified by *The Times* as "a pioneer in suitable frontage treatment for business needs"; it
was, in fact, the first office building in the modern tradition
in the city. Of interest here is the strong Chicago flavor, from
the gently curving cornice to the treatment of the two lower
stories. Equally important is the decorative enhancement of
the spandrels by ventilators. The handling of the building as a
whole, as base, shaft, and capital is quite Sullivanian, and
puts one in mind of a scaled-down Schiller or Wainwright
Building. Perhaps even more impressive in its mastery of the
commercial and industrial aesthetic is the Wallace Scott Fac-

tory of 1913–1916 in Glasgow (Figure 21). It reminds one of Albert Kahn at his best. On the basis of this evidence we would be inclined to say that Burnet was not only "a great stylist" as his contemporaries thought him to be but also one of the early masters of the Modern Movement.[16]

In the early 1920s Burnet expanded his London office to take on Tait and Francis Lorne as partners, and from this time onward the problem of identifying the hands of the individual designers is even more complicated. Lorne seems to have been responsible for a good many designs which were adaptations of Dudok. Burnet's last distinctively American building was probably Adelaide House, a large office building of 1921–1924 at the northern end of London Bridge (Figure 22). While the structural expression here is not so clear as in the Kodak building, the antecedents are undeniable. *The Times* remarked that it " . . . shows clearly its American origin of idea and scale." The last edifice on which Burnet is known to have worked is an office block in Glasgow at 200 St. Vincent Street done in 1929 (Figure 23). One would be hard put to find anything specifically American about it.

In view of the conventional picture of Burnet as a great stylist and in the light of his impeccable establishment credentials, this American element in his work is of considerable interest. It is appropriate to note here that in addition to his knighthood he received an LL.D. from the University of Glasgow and was a fellow of the R.I.B.A., from which he received a gold medal in 1923. He was also a corresponding member of the Institut de France, of the Société des architectes français, and of the A.I.A. During his lifetime he was known as perhaps the most French of English architects. His obituary in the *Journal of the Royal Institute of British Architects* remarked that " . . . in all Burnet's work there remained in evidence the influence of his Paris training in the twofold basis on which a scheme was from the first visualized, the layout in plan, and the materials and method of construction as applied to the practical requirements of

Figure 21
Sir John James Burnet,
Wallace Scott Factory,
Glasgow, 1913–1916

Figure 22
Burnet, Tait, and Lorne,
Adelaide House, London,
1921–1924

Figure 23
Sir John James Burnet,
office block at 200 St.
Vincent Street, Glasgow,
1929

the building under consideration."[17] This language is not only applicable to the principles of the Beaux-Arts; it is also a fair description of the theory of the Chicago School. We know that there was a strong element of French theory in the work of William Le Baron Jenney.[18] It is at least possible that Paris and Chicago were a good deal closer than is generally supposed. In his divided loyalty Burnet resembled a good many architects of his generation in both the United States and Europe. He is more than a little like D. H. Burnham.

The other major American contribution to British architecture in the pre–World War I era was Gordon Selfridge's exploitation of the steel frame in his famous department store. We hasten to add that Francis Swales, who was apparently the key designer for the first unit of the store, was *not* the first to use the steel frame in London. According to Nicholas Taylor, that honor belongs to the firm of Mewès and Davis, who employed it in the Ritz Hotel (1904–1906), the Morning Post building in Aldwych (1903–1907), and the Royal Automobile Club (1908–1911). The importance of Selfridge's Store lies in its owner's insistence on a wide bay system which could open up the interior so that all merchandise would be on display. That insistence can be understood only in terms of Selfridge's American experience.

Harry Gordon Selfridge (1856–1949) was perhaps the most gifted of all Marshall Field's partners. Having left the Field firm in 1903 to open his own store, he bought out the Schlesinger-Mayer Company, which had been in business in Chicago since 1872. After three months, unable to compete with Field's in good conscience, he sold his new concern to Carson, Pirie, Scott and Company. Financial particulars of this transaction are meager, but it is known that Selfridge was paid a premium or bonus of $150,000. In later years he liked to remark that he had bought the store from two Jews and sold it to seven Scotsmen, "all with beards, all of them Macs." More to the point here is the description of the building by his biographer as being one of twelve stories with broad open bays. This language precisely fits the famous structure designed by Louis Sullivan in 1899. It can reasonably be inferred that Selfridge was extremely familiar with the latest American innovations in department store design.

After a brief period of retirement in a palatial home built for him at Lake Geneva, Wisconsin, Selfridge decided to pursue an old dream and open a store in London. Ever since his first visit to the city, circa 1890, when he had been so overwhelmed by the textile and carpet designs of William Morris that he had cabled Marshall Field for permission to send an exhibition to Chicago, he had admired London and the English way of life. "This approval," says Reginald Pound, "did not extend to the London shops, which he thought antiquated."[19] In his new store he was determined to introduce American practice in every phase of the business. In architecture this determination was reinforced by his own personal fondness for the art. Architects' drawings were a favorite hobby, and his extensive personal library included many books on the subject.

As with all such establishments, the building history of Selfridge's is immensely complicated. The initial intention of Selfridge himself was to have the store designed by D. H. Burnham & Co., whom he knew well from his Chicago days. The Burnham office sent over a set of blueprints and a representative, Albert D. Miller. The plans, however, proved to be quite useless because of their non-adherence to English fire codes, which demanded a fire wall every forty feet. For some time this provision was the bane of Selfridge's existence. The noted publisher George H. Doran met Selfridge on a transatlantic crossing, "going out to Ohio solely to arrange for the purchase of numerous sheet-iron rolling partitions to enable him to comply with the London building ordinances." He objected to these archaic statutes because they interfered with his vision of spacious floors like those of Wertheim's in Berlin and Le Printemps in Paris. Pound writes:

He had seen what those limitations imposed on Harrods, whose store consisted of the juxtaposition of a series of compartments rather than departments. The insurance rates confirmed his opinion that the London regulations did not greatly reduce the fire risk.[20]

Largely as a result of Selfridge's struggle with the local authorities, some extremely desirable reforms were finally made in London's archaic building laws. One of the changed regulations was even referred to by contractors as "Selfridge's Act." His fight thus made possible a great quantity of later building in the city which utilized the steel frame more effectively. The present Oxford Street elevation of the store (Figure 24) is mostly the work of the previously mentioned Swales, who, however, was associated with the project for only a short time. The actual executors of the building were Robert F. Atkinson and Sir John Burnet, who were called in by Selfridge to adapt Burnham's plans. Nonetheless it was Swales to whom the credit (or blame) for the overpowering Greco-Roman facade must be assigned. In 1935 Selfridge himself wrote of Swales's drawing that "substantially, it was responsible for the house of Selfridge as it stands today."[21] The facade was, of course, perfectly in accord with Selfridge's own taste. Despite having lived in Chicago for thirty years during the most vital period of commercial architecture that the world has ever seen, he rejected its architectural innovations completely. In no way did he resemble his contemporary, Levi Z. Leiter (also at one time a Field partner), for whom William Le Baron Jenney did two of his finest buildings. A photograph taken in 1908 when the store was under construction (Figure 25) is a melancholy commentary on the manner in which the enormous columns—forty feet high, equaled only at the British Museum—mask the steel frame. Swales, of whom not much is known, later went on to do several hotels for the Canadian Pacific Railroad.

It is pertinent here to suggest that the conservatism of Selfridge's taste may perhaps be traced to his passionate desire to be accepted by the British aristocracy. This was

Figure 24
Robert F. Atkinson, Sir
John James Burnet, and
Francis Swales, Selfridge's
Store, London, 1908–1912

Figure 25
Robert F. Atkinson, Sir
John James Burnet, and
Francis Swales, Selfridge's
Store under construction,
London, 1908

a body not distinguished by any passion for architectural innovation, and Selfridge would naturally have tended to ape its tastes. It is indicative that he took frank delight in his tenancy of a town house from the Yarborough earls, with the Marquess of Salisbury and Lord Wimborne as his neighbors. The house itself contained numerous fine pictures, and his study was approached through a corridor filled with marble busts of eighteenth-century statesmen. Life at his country place, Highcliffe Castle, Hertfordshire, exhibited the same gracious, upper-class tone, and he also relished the cooperation of the College of Heralds in working out the extraordinary array of portcullises, shields, and checkers that adorned the store at the time of the 1911 coronation. The patrons of Voysey, who were probably the major supporters of architectural innovation in the Edwardian era, tended to come from a very different stratum of English society from the one that interested Selfridge. He rather resembled another Marshall Field executive, John G. Shedd, who encased his famous Chicago aquarium in a neoclassical shell.

In short, the American influence on British architecture in the pre–World War I period was substantial but ambivalent. While only C. H. Townsend responded to the powerful style of H. H. Richardson, several important figures were strongly influenced by McKim, Mead, and White, and in time Louis Sullivan, too, had an effect. In the long run the structural innovations forced by Gordon Selfridge were perhaps the most important of all. Without his example, the London fire code might have continued as an unreasonable restriction on the building industry.

Notes

1. Dudley A. Lewis, "Evaluations of American Architecture by European Critics, 1875–1900," Ph.D. thesis, University of Wisconsin, 1962.

2. Horace Townsend, "H. H. Richardson, Architect," *The Magazine of Art* 18 (1894): 133–138.

3. Henry-Russell Hitchcock, *The Architecture of H. H. Richardson and His Times* (New York, 1936), p. 284.

4. Nikolaus Pevsner, *Hertfordshire, The Buildings of England* (London, 1953), p. 77.

5. Robert Koch, "American Influence Abroad, 1886 and Later," *Journal of the Society of Architectural Historians* 18 (1959): 66–69.

6. Obituary Notice, "Charles Harrison Townsend," *The Builder,* 4 January, 1929, p. 30.

7. W. Fred, "Von englischer Baukunst," *Der Baumeister* 1 (1902): 18; *Die Arkitektur des XX Jahrhunderts* 1 (1901): 21.

8. *The Studio* 16 (1899): 196.

9. Ibid. 24 (1902): 198.

10. Henry-Russell Hitchcock has drawn the parallel between Glasgow and Chicago in "English Architecture in the Early 20th Century," *Zodiac* No. 18 (Milan, 1968), p. 7.

11. *The Book of the Liverpool School of Architecture,* ed. Lionel B. Budden (Liverpool and London, 1932), p. 27.

12. McKim, Mead & White, Miscellaneous Manuscripts, Box 3, New York Historical Society. John Brydon, a graduate of the office of Nesfield and Shaw and a prominent London practitioner in the 1890s, was also an admirer of the firm's work, especially of the Boston Public Library. I owe this reference to Mr. Richard G. Wilson.

13. Dr. Andor Gomme, personal communication to the author, 15 March 1969. I am indebted to Dr. Gomme and to his collaborator, David Walker, for much of the information contained in these paragraphs.

14. Alexander Paterson, "Sir John James Burnet," *Journal of the Royal Institute of British Architects* 31–32 (July 1938): 893–896.

15. Nicholas Taylor, "A Classic Case of Edwardianism," *The Architectural Review* 141 (1966): 17.

16. The role of Thomas Tait in the office in these years may have been extremely important. Sir John Summerson kindly has communicated to me his notes on a conversation with Tait at the Architectural Association on 3 May 1948: "*Kodak* Eastman wanted to do without a light well and to get as much light as possible from Kingsway. Tait made a design but Burnet didn't like it. So Tait's design and another were sent up and Tait's was chosen. The final design was worked out in the office. After that Tait did most of the designing." Tait also added that the nearby General Accident Building was "all Burnet's work."

17. Alexander Paterson, "Sir John James Burnet."

18. On the impact of Jenney's French training, see Theodore Turak, "The Ecole Centrale and Modern Architecture: The Education of

William Le Baron Jenney," *Journal of the Society of Architectural Historians* 29 (1970): 40–47.

19. Reginald Pound, *Selfridge* (London, 1960), p. 28. I have relied on this book, which is in the nature of an authorized biography, for many details of the Selfridge career.

20. Ibid., p. 36.

21. Ibid., p. 39.

3

Karl Moser
and the German
Richardsonian

"Pleasing and instructive, indeed," wrote a German critic in
1899, "are the buildings dating from about the middle of the
seventies, when Richardson, by that splendid architectural
achievement, the Trinity Church of Boston, had succeeded
in emancipating American architecture from the trammels of
European tradition." The author, Leopold Gmelin, continued
in the same vein:

It is true that Richardson, like his predecessors, drew
largely upon European models for his material, and based
his work upon Romanic [sic] forms borrowed from the Norman and the Provençal styles. Nevertheless, his creations
bear an imprint so characteristic, and accord so fully with
modern demands, as to justify the opinion, on the part of
European architects, that he should be regarded as the
founder of an independent style of architecture in the New
World. The foreign artist instinctively feels that Richardson
must have been possessed of greater creative genius than
any of his predecessors on the American continent. Primitive strength, noble simplicity, monumental grandeur, un-
wavering rectitude, and a lofty disdain of all petty embel-
lishments are the attributes perpetuated in Richardson's
work. The professional European visitor passes by the older
specimens of American architecture with indifference,
for they compare unfavorably with their European prototypes; but when he comes upon one of Richardson's masterpieces he stands spellbound and mute with admiration. [1]

While this quotation is undoubtedly somewhat effusive
in tone, it is representative of a large body of German opinion
about American architecture in the 1890s.

So much has been written about the significance of Ernest
Wasmuth's 1910 publication of Frank Lloyd Wright's work in
Berlin that one would tend to think the Germans were quite
unaware of American work prior to that date. In point of
fact, no opinion could be farther from the truth. Imperial
Germany was unquestionably the most dynamic state in
Europe, bent on expansion in the cultural, economic, and
political spheres. It was intent on demonstrating German
superiority in all fields, and it spared no pains to inform
itself on the progress of its competitors. One aspect of the
national program was a network of technical attachés, sta-
tioned in the capitals of the leading powers and commis-

sioned to report on developments in their fields. Of these
undoubtedly the best known was Hermann Muthesius, whose
Das englische Haus (Berlin, 1908) remains the best work on
English domestic architecture of the period. More important
in our context, however, was Karl Hinckeldeyn, attaché at
the Washington embassy from 1884 to 1887. He played a
key role in the German appreciation of Richardson.

Born at Lübeck in 1847, Hinckeldeyn attended the famous
Bauakademie in Berlin and entered the service of the German state in 1877. Prior to his Washington assignment he
was assistant editor of the influential *Zentralblatt der
Bauverwaltung,* and hence in close touch with the progress
of the building industry. His experience in this country re-
sulted in a remarkable series of articles on American architecture in German publications. He was, as Dudley Lewis
has noted, one of the foremost interpreters of American
trends in Europe and certainly the most prolific German
writer on the subject. In general he stressed two points:
(1) the livability of American dwellings and (2) the originality
and power of H. H. Richardson. With regard to the latter
point, it should be noted that Hinckeldeyn arrived in the
United States at the very moment when Richardson was at
the zenith of his fame. He could hardly have failed to be impressed by the poll of 1885, and the following year he wrote
an extremely respectful obituary of Richardson for the
Zentralblatt.[2]

In the next decade Hinckeldeyn wrote a number of excellent articles on various aspects of American architecture
for German professional journals. His work culminated in
1897 in his collaboration with Paul Graef on the remarkable
volume *Neubauten in Nordamerika,* published by Julius
Becker in Berlin. This book, for which he wrote a short but
perceptive introduction, contained a hundred plates, most
of them of exceptional quality. Perhaps the most interesting
aspect of the work is its concentration upon architecture in a
Richardsonian vein. A fair estimate would be that about

three-quarters of the edifices shown were of this character. Thus the firm of Holabird & Roche was represented not by the Tacoma Building or any of their other office structures in the Chicago Loop but by the Physics Building of 1886 at Northwestern University, which was essentially another version of Richardson's Sever Hall at Harvard (Figures 26 and 27); similarly the Detroit firm of Mason and Rice, for which Albert Kahn worked in the 1890s, was represented by an extremely Richardsonian Y.M.C.A. building of 1883 (Figure 28), and Bruce Price by a gatehouse built in 1889–1890 at Tuxedo Park, New York, which continues the line of development staked out by Richardson in his Ames Gate Lodge of 1880 (Figure 29). As Lewis has pointed out, this selection was misleading. Price, for example, had already in 1892 moved over to the French Renaissance manner in his Château Frontenac Hotel for the Canadian Pacific Railroad. The authors showed no building by Louis Sullivan and none by McKim, Mead & White. Hinckeldeyn was among those European critics who viewed the neoclassicism of the Chicago World's Fair as a catastrophe, and the picture of American architecture that he offered to his German readers was of his old hero, Richardson, as a continuing vital force.

The depth of his regard for Richardson was again demonstrated in 1905 when a second edition of the work appeared, this time from the Max Spielmayer Verlag. This later version featured sixty-five additional illustrations, including no less than ten buildings by the master himself. They were

1. The State Capitol, Albany, New York
2. The Gratwick house, Buffalo, New York
3. The Town Hall, North Easton, Massachusetts
4. The Ames Memorial Library, North Easton, Massachusetts
5. The Crane Library, Quincy, Massachusetts
6. The John Hay house, Washington, D.C.
7. The Allegheny County buildings, Pittsburgh, Pennsylvania
8. Austin Hall, Cambridge, Massachusetts

Figure 26
Holabird & Roche, Physics
Building, Northwestern
University, 1886

Figure 27
H. H. Richardson, Sever
Hall, Harvard University,
1878–1880

Figure 28
Mason and Rice, Y.M.C.A.
Building, Detroit, 1883

Figure 29
Bruce Price, Gate Lodge,
Tuxedo Park, New York,
1889–1890

Figure 30
H. H. Richardson, doorway
of John Hay house,
Washington, D.C., 1884.
Plate from *Neubauten in
Nordamerika,* Berlin, 1905

9. The Billings Library, Burlington, Vermont

10. The MacVeagh house, Chicago, Illinois.

Once again most of the photographs were of excellent quality, and some of them, such as the picture of the entryway
to the John Hay house (Figure 30) were really superb. As in
1897, a great many plans were included, and building costs
were also generally supplied. To an amazing extent the
Richardsonian achievement was communicated to the German architectural public, and it is significant that the
publicist himself had by this time achieved considerable eminence. In 1902 Karl Hinckeldeyn became president of the
Berlin Akademie der Bauwesen and in 1903, minister director. It is not too much to say that in Germany Richardson
had strong official sponsorship, and it is not surprising that
in certain German cities there was, as Carroll Meeks noted
several years ago, a remarkable outbreak of Richardsonian
architecture around the year 1900.[3] The centers of this
German Richardsonian were Mannheim and Karlsruhe, and
its chief exponents were the firm of Curjel and Moser.

Karl Moser (1860–1936) was the designing partner and
the third in line of what must be one of the most remarkable
architectural dynasties on the European continent. His
grandfather was a Swiss stonemason and architect. His
father, Robert Moser, was a successful architect who studied
with Eisenlohr in Karlsruhe and did a series of government
buildings in Baden and Aargau. His son, Werner Moser
(1898–1970), was a student of Frank Lloyd Wright and one
of the leading Swiss architects of his generation. His grand-
son, Lorenz Moser, continues the family tradition of architectural practice in Switzerland today. All the Mosers have
apparently possessed a good deal of personal charm, which
is not, however, in any way incompatible with substantial
force of character. Karl Moser is probably best known for
his courageous role as juror in the famous League of Nations
competition of 1927 and for his powerful St. Anton's Roman
Catholic Church in Basel of 1925–1927. This edifice broke

radically with the existing traditions of church design in Switzerland; it was, in fact, the first wholly modern church in the country. Though somewhat overlooked today, it should be ranked as one of the best buildings of the 1920s (Figures 31 and 32).

With a strong family background in architecture, it was natural for Karl Moser to attend the Eidgenössische Technische Hochschule in Zurich. After graduation in 1878, he went to Paris for advanced study at the Ecole des Beaux-Arts; it does not appear, however, that this French experience had any very deep effect upon him. Following a period of practical training in Baden and Wiesbaden, he made a *Studienreise* to Italy in 1887, and the next year he formed a partnership with Robert Curjel in Karlsruhe. This association lasted until 1915, when Moser returned to Zurich to take up a professorship at his old school. In many respects the atmosphere in Karlsruhe was congenial for the young firm. It was one of the newest and least historical cities in Germany. There was no collection of Gothic gables and towers to inhibit the architect. A contemporary writer actually noted the existence of "American conditions" in the town.[4] Like many German provincial centers in the Wilhelmian Reich, this small city exhibited a lively cultural life. One thinks immediately of the grand ducal court at Darmstadt and its patronage of Joseph Olbrich in the buildings on the Mathildenhöhe. Similarly Henry van de Velde owed much to a grand duke (who was not nearly so attractive a personality as the Darmstadt ruler) for his support of the Kunstgewerbeschule at Weimar, the predecessor of the Bauhaus. In Karlsruhe the cultural scene was graced by several prominent figures, the best known of whom was perhaps Felix Mottl, the famous Wagnerian conductor. A notable municipal art gallery with outstanding examples of the work of Grünewald was also built up in these years. The atmosphere, however, was never so progressive as in Darmstadt and Weimar. Moser's biographer remarks that the young architects of

Karlsruhe around the turn of the century were not united but were agreed that historical forms should not be copied. They should be freely interpreted in personal variations. This situation had a good deal to do with Moser's development.[5] We must emphasize the importance of these provincial centers in the development of architecture in Wilhelmian Germany. Very often they espoused tendencies that were quite contrary to those fostered by the regime in Berlin.

The first overtly Richardsonian building by Curjel and Moser was the Pauluskirche in Basel (Figures 33 and 34). This structure was built between June 1898 and November 1901 and was therefore probably designed in the winter of 1897-1898. (Note the close correlation with the appearance of *Neubauten in Nordamerika.*) The plan is a Greek cross with a close resemblance to that of Trinity Church in Boston, Richardson's early masterpiece, which had already been published in Germany in Hinckeldeyn's obituary in the *Zentralblatt der Bauverwaltung.* The tower in the center is short and stubby with turrets at the corners; it has a considerable resemblance to Stanford White's tower for Trinity. For this feature no iron reinforcements were used, an indication of the soundness in construction that characterized the entire job; in looking at the buildings of Curjel and Moser one usually has the feeling that they were put together with exceptional care. In this case the base and steps of the edifice were granite, and the exterior was the coarse red sandstone that is common in Basel. A contemporary German writer observed that the Pauluskirche was " . . . a proof that churches professedly archaic and complete in all details of the Romanesque style can yet bear the addition of modern touches, without sacrificing any of their sacredness."[6] The church is, of course, even less Romanesque than Trinity. The rose window on the western elevation is an element that the Boston church does not possess, but it is interesting to note that Richardson used such fenestration in a perspective study in 1873.

Figure 31
Karl Moser, St. Anton's
Roman Catholic Church,
Basel, Switzerland, 1925–
1927

Figure 32
Karl Moser, interior, St.
Anton's Roman Catholic
Church, Basel, Switzerland,
1925–1927

Figure 34
Curjel and Moser, detail of
tower, Pauluskirche, Basel,
Switzerland, 1897–1898

Figure 33
Curjel and Moser,
Pauluskirche, Basel,
Switzerland, 1897–1898

Figure 36
Fischer and Patton, Beloit
College Chapel, Beloit,
Wisconsin, 1893. Plate
from *Neubauten in
Nordamerika,* Berlin, 1905

Figure 37
Curjel and Moser, St.
Johanniskirche, Mannheim,
1900–1901

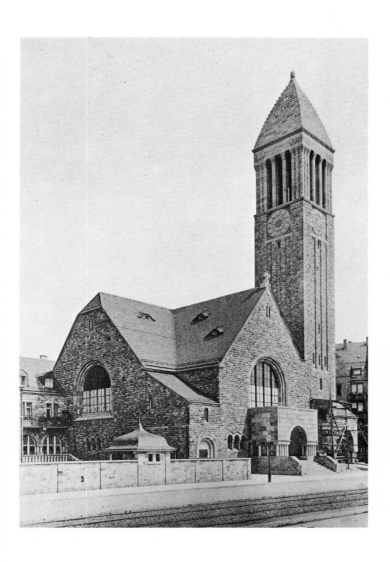

Figure 38
Curjel and Moser,
Lutherkirche, Karlsruhe,
1905–1906

Figure 39
Curjel and Moser, Parish
House, Lutherkirche,
Karlsruhe, 1905–1906

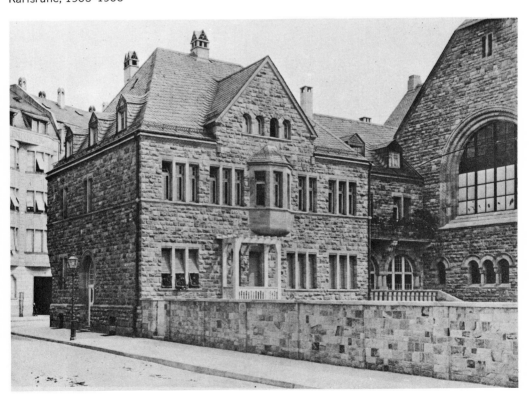

In 1901 Curjel and Moser began the construction of the St. Johanniskirche in Mannheim. For this project the original prototype was probably Richardson's Brattle Square Church of 1870–1872, but the immediate model must have been the Beloit College Chapel of 1893 by Patton and Fischer of Chicago (Figures 35, 36, and 37) which had appeared as plate number 28 in *Neubauten.* The massing of the two structures is too similar to be disregarded, and in both the plans is a simple Greek cross. The corner towers are also very close, and in both the principal elevation is opened up with a triplicated arch; in Mannheim a porte cochere was also added, as was a parsonage. The latter element is lacking at Beloit.[7] Whereas the American building was constructed of a characteristic rock-faced Richardsonian granite, Curjel and Moser used a white sandstone from the Palatinate that was rusticated to achieve the same general effect. The carved ornament in the tower is not at all Richardsonian, but, like that on the Pauluskirche in Basel, relates to the contemporary Jugend movement, to which the firm would subscribe in 1907.

It is not too much to say that the Johanniskirche became a kind of ideogram on which Curjel and Moser played a series of variations during the next few years. Of these the largest was probably the Lutherkirche on the Melanchthonplatz in Karlsruhe, designed in 1904–1905 (Figure 38). Here a type of triumphal arch was substituted for the arcade on the western elevation, but the basic form remained the same. The parish house (Figure 39) is in this case even more Richardsonian than the church itself; with its group of square-headed windows and its oriel, it might be mistaken for a building of the 1890s in almost any American city. Equally striking is a semicircular element that projects from the rear of the parish house. This is a feature which can be found in much of Richardson's domestic work and which was also used by Wright in his Winslow house of 1893. In the nineteenth century the spaces formed by such an enclosure often served as solariums; in the case of the Winslow house, however, the projecting bay was a tiny music room. Overall the impression of the Lutherkirche and its parish house is strongly Richardsonian. The attraction of the form is suggested by the remark of the editors of *Architektur des zwanzigstern Jahrhunderts* that the church " . . . is built in the Romanesque style, and resembles in character the greater number of modern Protestant churches."[8]

The last in the series of Richardsonian churches by Curjel and Moser was the St. Antonkirche in Zurich, built 1906–1908 (Figures 40, 41, and 42); here the triumphal arch was maintained at the entry but the position of the tower was reversed. The walling was the same rock-faced ashlar, a somewhat unfamiliar building material in Zurich. In this entire series of buildings we should particularly note the importance of surface texture; it is one of the most strongly Richardsonian elements in the design. In one respect the plan was unlike the examples in Mannheim and Karlsruhe; the architects used a strongly articulated transept culminating in a conical form rather like the termination that Richardson had used at the Billings Library in Burlington, Vermont. The porte cochere was used once again, and here the detailing of the capitals has a considerable resemblance to the stubby Byzantine form that Richardson had used in Austin Hall at Harvard University. This is probably the firm's most Richardsonian church, and it is noteworthy that its design date coincides with the 1905 publication of Graef and Hinckeldeyn's *Neubauten,* which included a fine series of photographs of Austin Hall (Figures 43 and 44). It is hard to escape the conclusion that Curjel and Moser were familiar with this book.

While the firm used the Richardsonian Romanesque mainly for church buildings, it also executed a few secular structures in this manner. Of these the most important was the Bankhaus Homburger in Karlsruhe, built 1898–1901 (Figure 45). Here the site problem was close to the one that Richardson had faced in his Ames Building of 1882–1883 (Figure 46).

Figure 40
Curjel and Moser, St.
Antonkirche, Zurich,
1906–1908

Figure 41
Curjel and Moser, St.
Antonkirche, side elevation
and transept, Zurich,
1906–1908

Figure 42
Curjel and Moser, St.
Antonkirche, detail of porte
cochere, Zurich, 1906–1908

Figure 43
H. H. Richardson, Austin
Hall, Harvard University,
1881–1883. Plate from
Neubauten in Nordamerika,
Berlin, 1905.

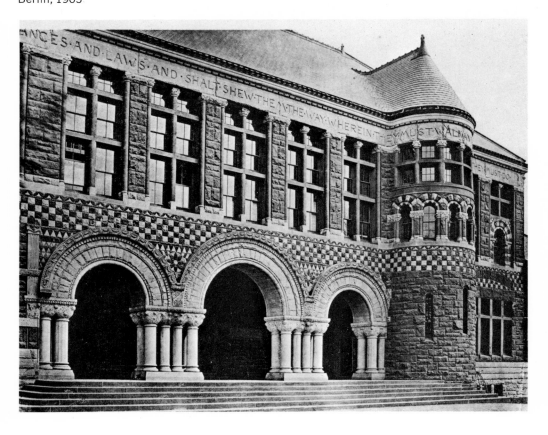

Figure 44
H. H. Richardson, Austin
Hall, detail of capital,
Harvard University, 1881–
1883. Plate from *Neubauten
in Nordamerika,* Berlin,
1905

Figure 45
Curjel and Moser,
Bankhaus Homburger,
Karlsruhe, 1898–1901

Figure 46
H. H. Richardson, Ames
Building, Boston, 1881–
1883

Figure 47
Curjel and Moser, dwelling
house, Hofstrasse,
Karlsruhe, 1898–1901

Curjel and Moser confronted a corner lot that was shaped like a piece of pie. Their solution was an elevation composed of strongly detailed bays under round arches; in this manner the difficult corner was skillfully turned. At the top is a series of dormers, also Richardsonian in derivation. The structure is massively built of yellowish white Spessart sandstone. Though the interior has been much altered, the building still stands today, as does the Lutherkirche.

In these same years 1898–1901 the firm also built several dwelling houses in Karlsruhe. Of these the largest was probably at Number 2 Hofstrasse (Figure 47). It, too, contained several Richardsonian elements, but the total composition was unhappily quite disorganized. It is perhaps no great loss that this building no longer survives; it was probably a casualty of the Second World War, in which the city was heavily bombed. A very similar edifice, now a dancing academy, is located a few blocks away.

Here we must confront the difficult but important question of distinguishing the Richardsonian manner of Curjel and Moser from the contemporary Romanesque revival in Germany. More than any other European nation, nineteenth-century Germany was attached to Romanesque forms in its architecture. The sources of this attachment can be found in the romantic medievalism that was so much a part of German nationalism and of the drive for unification under the leadership of Prussia. From 1800 onward German artists and intellectuals generally looked backward longingly at the medieval past, and the period on which they tended to concentrate was the Hohenstaufen empire of the twelfth and thirteenth centuries. Germany under the Hohenstaufens had been strong and united, a powerful voice in the councils of Europe. Their object in the politics of their own day was the restoration of such a state of affairs. Naturally there was an intense interest in the art and architecture of this glorious bygone age. Renewed attention was paid to the ancient legend of the Kyffhäuser, the magic mountain in Thuringia where Friedrich

Barbarossa was supposedly buried, and a Romanesque mausoleum was seen as the only possible burial place for a hero of the German Reich. Schiller, Goethe, and Bismarck were all, in fact, interred in Romanesque tombs.[9]

Hence we find, from about 1850 onward, a large number of important buildings of a decidedly Romanesque character. These can usually be quite easily differentiated from the earlier *Rundbogenstil* on the basis of associational values and archeological correctness. The center of this wave of revivalism was the valley of the Rhine, the traditional heartland of German Catholicism. It was, and is, an area rich in medieval remains. In fact, the Germans justified much of their early neo-Romanesque work as extensions to medieval churches. The first neo-Romanesque basilica in the Rhineland, built at Stieldorf in 1850 by Ernst Friedrich Zwirner, was connected to a twelfth-century tower. The single most important source for this Rhenish Romanesque was undoubtedly the cathedral of Speyer, which it will be noted, had significant associations with the Hohenstaufen dynasty; founded by Emperor Conrad II in 1030, it was the burial place of eight members of the line (Figures 48 and 49). The impact of this great building can be readily seen in works such as the church of St. Elizabeth in Bonn, which, after a somewhat confused competition, was built by Ludwig Becker between 1903 and 1912 (Figures 50, 51, 52, and 53). While this structure unquestionably owes its tripartite portal and certain features of its western tower to Speyer, it also includes elements from a variety of other sources. Thus the choir is dependent upon other Rhenish examples, especially Münstermaifeld and Sinzig, and the interior arcades are modeled on those of the Abbey Church of Mönchen-Gladbach. There is none of this archeologizing in Curjel and Moser, or for that matter, in Richardson himself, who, after Trinity Church, hardly ever referred to a specific medieval precedent.[10]

We should note that from the point of view of German Catholicism the Romanesque style had much in its favor. It was unquestionably a Christian style; moreover it was viewed as an uncompleted style and was therefore susceptible of further development. Finally, it could be interpreted as a distinctly German style, and in a period when the church was under attack by Bismarck's *Kulturkampf,* this was no mean advantage. Even such a progressive critic as Gottfried Semper, who was concerned with practical questions of acoustics and visibility for Protestant churches, felt that the Romanesque style, more than the Gothic, should be retained because of its associations with the German past. On the whole, however, in the Rhenish neo-Romanesque, we have a revival style with nothing of Richardson about it.

The picture changes and becomes much more complicated with the accession of Wilhelm II to the German throne in 1888. After this date the Romanesque revival became to a remarkable extent an *imperial* style, closely identified with the ambitions of the house of Hohenzollern. The ground had been prepared for this development earlier in the century by a number of writers and intellectuals. In 1848 the great historian Johann Gustav Droysen, then teaching at the University of Kiel, declared, "To the Hohenzollern belongs the place which has been empty since the days of the Hohenstaufen."[11] It was completely natural, then, for the new German empire of 1871 to adopt as an official style the architecture that could evoke the great days of the Imperial Reich under the Hohenstaufens. In court circles it was felt that government buildings should be an embodiment of the concept of the state. It was wholly appropriate for the administration of Wilhelm I to undertake the restoration of the cathedrals of Mainz, Worms, and Speyer, and of the imperial palace at Goslar, certain portions of which may be the sources for the rock-faced ashlar that was much favored by German architects at the end of the century.

When Wilhelm II ascended the throne in 1888, his first message to the nation included the famous sentence "The King's will is the supreme law of the land." What is not usually

Figure 48
Speyer Cathedral, begun
1025–1030

Figure 49
Speyer Cathedral, rear
elevation, begun 1025–
1030

Figure 50
Ludwig Becker, Church of
St. Elizabeth, Bonn, 1903–
1912

Figure 51
Ludwig Becker, tower,
Church of St. Elizabeth,
Bonn, 1903–1912

Figure 52
Ludwig Becker, doorway,
Church of St. Elizabeth,
Bonn, 1903–1912

Figure 53
Ludwig Becker, detail of
apse, Church of St.
Elizabeth, Bonn, 1903–
1912

Figure 54
Franz Schwechten,
Kaiserschloss, Posen,
1909–1910

Figure 55
Franz Schwechten, *Festsaal*
of Kaiserschloss, Posen,
1909–1910. From a paint-
ing by Marno Kellner

noticed is that his overwhelming ambition to extend the royal authority encompassed the field of architecture. The Kaiser very definitely thought of himself as an arbiter of taste. He hated the manner that Henry van de Velde was developing in Weimar and went out of his way to insult that artist in a famous episode at the ducal court. The story is bitterly recounted in van de Velde's autobiography. As Albert Speer has recently remarked, the Kaiser's own personal preference was for the incredibly pompous neobaroque of his private architect Eberhard von Ihne — a taste that was carried on in many of the buildings of the Nazi regime. For government buildings, however, there was nothing like the neo-Romanesque, which symbolized the glories of the Hohenstaufen regime and the continuity of the new empire with the imperial past.

In the Wilhelmian building program, then, we find a large number of structures that are generally Romanesque in character but never as archeological as the churches of the Rhineland. Sometimes there will be a quotation from the cathedral of Speyer or the palace at Goslar, and in a few instances a Richardsonian detail may creep in. There is, however, no relationship to identifiable Richardsonian models, as in the work of Curjel and Moser. Almost always the decorative elements will have an imperial reference. An especially interesting example is the colossal Kaiserschloss of 1905–1910 in Posen by Professor Franz Schwechten (Figures 54 and 55). This immense pile is a mélange of Romanesque elements: arcades, towers, and monumental doorways are all here. The walling is a rough-cut ashlar, which might be thought of as a Richardsonian material, but here it is not used in a way typical of the American master. Particularly intriguing is the decorative program of the great *Festsaal,* or reception hall. In Wilhelmian architecture interior wall treatments were intended to carry through the architectural statements made on the exterior of the building. Here a series of mosaics show the Hohenstaufen emperors in the complete imperial regalia, with robe, crown, orb, and scepter. The design of the throne, which rests on a pair of elephants, can be traced to an eleventh-century example in the cathedral of Canossa, also a city closely associated with the Hohenstaufens. The iconography could hardly be clearer.[12]

In keeping with his concept of himself as arbiter of taste, the Kaiser sometimes actively intervened in government building projects. In an office building in Bonn of 1903–1906 he actually added a tower at the northeast corner. Another structure in which he took an intense personal interest was the 1904 glass factory of Puhl and Wagner, also by Franz Schwechten. Thoroughly Romanesque in style, it makes an interesting comparison to the Fagus shoe last factory at Alfeld an der Leine, done by Gropius and Meyer in 1911. There is, of course, a great deal of this Imperial Romanesque in Berlin in buildings associated with the court. It also occurred in those portions of the empire where there was a large non-German population. Here it was a means of "showing the flag." The Metz railroad station of 1902–1905 by Jürgen Kröger (Figures 56 and 57), which was the writer's introduction to the style, is a good case in point. Some of the detailing, as in the eyebrow dormers of the corner pavilion, is Richardsonian, but on the whole the sources of the building lie in German medieval precedent. Like the Kaiserschloss in Posen (now Poznan), it is an assertion of the presence of German power in an area where the authorities were uneasy.[13]

The importance of the relatively free atmosphere of Karlsruhe and Mannheim for Curjel and Moser now becomes clear. It enabled them to produce Romanesque buildings with very little of the ideological baggage that is so noticeable in the work of Schwechten, Kröger, and the other official architects of the Wilhelmian regime. It is, in fact, not surprising that they turned for models to Richardson, an architect in whose work symbolic content is at a minimum.

Figure 56
Jürgen Kröger, railroad
station, Metz, 1905

Figure 57
Jürgen Kröger, corner
pavilion, railroad station,
Metz, 1902–1905

Figure 58
Curjel and Moser, Kunst-
haus, Zurich, 1907–1910

Figure 59
Curjel and Moser, wall
detail, Kunsthaus, Zurich,
1907–1910

Figure 60
Curjel and Moser, interior
court, University of Zurich,
1910

Figure 61
Curjel and Moser, University
of Zurich, 1910

To Curjel and Moser it must have appeared that Richardson and his followers had simply used the Romanesque as a basis for the development of a truly contemporary style. It was a Romanesque revival without a heavy ideological content, and that is what they themselves were trying to obtain. Alan Gowans has noted that "neither archeology nor symbolism motivated Richardson's predilection for Romanesque. . . . So little interest had he in the style for its own sake that it is doubtful if in all his years in Paris he even visited the Romanesque country of southern France."[14] His style thus suited Curjel and Moser to a remarkable degree.

On a deeper level it is likely that the Richardsonian Romanesque was for Curjel and Moser, as it was for Eliel Saarinen and Lars Sonck, a kind of bridge style between the historicism of the nineteenth century and the manner that was developing in the hands of Olbrich, van de Velde, Behrens, and a variety of others. A parallel case might be made to explain the Romanesque backgrounds that occur in certain fifteenth-century paintings, notably Jan van Eyck's Ghent altarpiece, "The Adoration of the Mystic Lamb." In these works one feels that the Romanesque architecture is a kind of transition element toward a development sensed but not as yet fully understood. It disappears in the work of Rogier van der Weyden and the later Flemish painters of the fifteenth century. Similarly the overtly Romanesque elements drop out of Curjel and Moser's work in 1907 in the design for the Kunsthaus in Zurich (Figures 58, 59). Here the wall detailing is smooth and polished with a rather classical flavor. There is nothing of the Richardsonian quality which is so characteristic of the work in Karlsruhe. The same can be said of the first building for the University of Zurich, which was done at almost the same time (Figures 60, 61). In short the inspiration of the Richardsonian Romanesque was for Curjel and Moser a vital but short-lived phase.

Why, then, did the most promising young German architects active around 1910 see Frank Lloyd Wright as the first American architect of international significance? It is quite clear that this was the view of Walter Gropius (1883-1969) and Mies van der Rohe (1886–1969). The answer to this question probably lies in the German literature on the subject. After the outburst of enthusiasm for Richardson in the 1890s and early years of the century, German architectural editors generally followed Hinckeldeyn in believing that American architecture had succumbed to a wave of sterile neoclassicism. The view of *Moderne Bauformen,* which was published in Stuttgart, was typical. This periodical was probably more international in its coverage than any other German magazine of the pre-World War I period. It devoted extensive space to the work of Voysey in England and Saarinen, Gesellius, and Lindgren in Helsinki. As one searches its volumes for the years 1900–1914, he looks in vain for any mention of equally exciting work in the United States. The image of American work that *Moderne Bauformen* projected is well reflected in a review of John Cordis Baker, *American Country Homes and Their Gardens* (Philadelphia, 1906), which appeared in the June 1907 issue. It was copiously illustrated with photographs of country places by McKim, Mead & White, Charles Platt, and Wilson Eyre. The reviewer, Paul Schultze-Naumburg, who was one of the most distinguished scholars of his generation, and later a leading Nazi, not unnaturally concluded that the orientation of American architects who were working in this field, which Hinckeldeyn had found so vital, was primarily neoclassical.

A second excellent example of the German attitude toward American architecture in the Wilhelmian years is to be found in *Das moderne Landhaus und seine innere Ausstattung* (Munich, 1905) by the indefatigable Hermann Muthesius. In his introduction Muthesius observed that the modern country house was an essentially new architectural problem. It was a result of the growth of the modern city and was basically a place in which to escape from the pressures of urban life. His analysis of the complex questions of planning, heating, ventilating, and so on, is excellent. Most relevant here, however, is Muthesius' choice of examples. The largest number of his 320 illustrations were taken, as might be expected, from Germany and Austria, and they included houses by Peter Behrens, Theodor Fischer, Alfred Messel, Josef Olbrich, and Josef Hofmann. He also showed interiors and furniture by the excellent cabinetmaker Bruno Paul. From England he chose fine examples by Voysey, George Walton, and Baillie Scott, and there is an exceptional series of plates showing the work of Mackintosh. Finland was represented by Eliel Saarinen's own villa outside Helsinki, which was shown in considerable detail. The American selection, however, was composed of houses by Wilson Eyre, Alfred Cookman Cass, W. E. Jackson, Wyatt and Nolting, Grosvenor Atterbury, and Alfred Hoyt Granger. It can hardly be claimed that any of these dwellings was of much distinction.

Even more striking is the analysis of the American architectural scene offered by F. Rudolph Vogel in *Das amerikanische Haus* (Berlin, 1910). This lengthy volume, with 285 pages and ample illustration, was published by the Wasmuth Verlag, which had also been responsible for the books of Muthesius. There is at least some possibility that it was intended to be a companion piece to the earlier very successful *Das englische Haus.* In many ways Vogel's book is an excellent work. He obviously traveled widely, met a great many architects, and did his best to acquaint himself with the country's most significant monuments. On the historical side his research was as thorough as it could have been at the time. It is remarkable to find him devoting several pages to the role of the ill-fated William Rimmer of Boston in the seventies and eighties. On the other hand, Vogel was evidently by nature a rather conservative person. From his text it is clear that he was out of sympathy with the latest developments in the architecture of his own country. Thus he did not evaluate the Chicago World's Fair of 1893 as a disaster for architecture but as a stimulus for park and city planning. He noted that four years after the exposition Cleveland was beginning to improve its river banks and that Harrisburg, Washington, and Baltimore were doing the same. Buffalo, Boston, Charleston, and Chicago were likewise formulating park plans in the early years of the century. It is suggestive that in his introduction he particularly mentions his indebtedness to eastern architects, notably Wilson Eyre and Carrère & Hastings. He continues the Hinckeldeyn tradition of reverence for Richardson but sees Adler and Sullivan merely as followers, showing only their Auditorium Hotel of 1886–1888. In the final chapter, which is a survey of contemporary trends, he shows the Winslow, Willits, and Husser houses by Wright, but without plans, sections, or details; much more attention is devoted to large country houses by Peabody and Stearns, Carrère & Hastings, and Horace Trumbauer. There is no evidence that Vogel understood the significance of Wright's work. In this respect there is an interesting contrast to Hugo Koch's *Gartenkunst im Städtebau* (Berlin, 1914), a book that laid the achievement of Jens Jensen before the European public at a time when Jensen was almost unknown outside the Chicago area. [15]

It is, of course, impossible to evaluate the influence of any one of these publications on the generation of young German architects who were coming to maturity in the years just prior to the First World War, but their cumulative impact must have been substantial. The book of Vogel may have been especially important because of the great prestige of the Wasmuth Verlag. For men like Walter Gropius and Mies van der Rohe the image of American architecture that was presented here was anything but exciting. It would have appeared to them as caught up in a different version of the same historicism that was so prevalent in their own country. The work of polished society architects such as Eyre and Trumbauer would certainly have compared unfavorably with the vital creations of Behrens, Olbrich, Mackintosh,

or Saarinen. For Gropius and Mies the architecture of the
United States would have appeared, to put the matter gently,
to have taken an unfortunate turn. In order to obtain a dif-
ferent picture of what was going on in the United States they
would have had to be familiar with the treatment of Wright
and the Prairie School in *The Architectural Review* (Boston),
The Architectural Record, or perhaps *The Ladies' Home
Journal* and *House Beautiful.* It is unlikely that many young
German architects had access to these journals. Hence the
Wasmuth folio of 1910, with its exceptionally handsome
renderings, many of them the work of Marion Mahoney
Griffin, must have been a remarkable shock. It is perhaps
indicative of its impact that in 1912 *Moderne Bauformen*
published the Carl Schurz High School by Dwight Perkins.
This building, one of the real masterpieces of the Prairie
School, was done in 1908–1910. If war had not intervened,
German magazines might have shown a good many similar
structures.

Concerning the impact of the Wasmuth folio on European
architecture a great deal has already been written. In addition to Mies and Gropius themselves, Sigfried Giedion,
Bruno Zevi, James Fitch, and Peter Blake have discussed
the question at various points in their writings, and there
is no need to go into it here. It must be emphasized, however,
that in turning to Wright, Mies and Gropius were not the first
German architects to go to American work for inspiration.
They were, in fact, merely resuming a custom that had
dropped out of use for a few years.

Notes

1. Leopold Gmelin, "American Architecture from a German
Point of View," *The Forum* 27 (1899): 700. This article is an amplification of an earlier publication in *Deutsche Bauzeitung,* 1895.
Gmelin was evidently one of the large number of German architects
who came to the United States for the 1893 World's Fair.

2. Dudley Lewis, "Karl Hinckeldeyn: Critic of American Architecture," *The American-German Review* 27 (1960–1961): 10–14.

3. Carroll Meeks, *The Railroad Station* (New Haven, 1956), p. 137.

4. Karl Widmer, "Die Moderne Karlsruher Architektenschule," *Der Baumeister* 4 (1905–1906): 53–56.

5. Herman Kienzle, *Karl Moser 1860–1936* (Zurich, 1937). This brief monograph is the last work on Moser. He awaits his biographer.

6. *Architektur des zwanzigsten Jahrhunderts,* vol. 2 (Berlin, 1902), p. 9. The text is in English, French, and German. This is the English version, not a translation.

7. Normand S. Patton (1852–1915) was one of the leading Richardsonian designers in the Midwest. Among his most important works were the Chicago Theological Seminary, The Kalamazoo Public Library, and a high school in Muskegon, Michigan. In his late work he moved away from Richardson to a neoclassical manner much like that of McKim, Mead & White. Patton's buildings were frequently published in *The Inland Architect,* and he was a director of the A.I.A. from 1896 to 1902.

8. *Architektur des zwanzigsten Jahrhunderts,* vol. 8 (Berlin, 1908), p. 13.

9. On the intellectual background of nineteenth-century Germany, Hans Kohn, *The Mind of Germany* (New York, 1960) is extremely useful. I have relied on it extensively.

10. For the analysis of the church of St. Elizabeth, and for much other information, I am indebted to the excellent Ph.D. thesis of Dr. Michael Bringmann, "Studien zur neuromanischen Architektur in Deutschland" (Heidelberg, 1968).

11. Kohn, *Mind of Germany,* p. 5.

12. The throne is described and pictured on pp. 8–13 of an article by André Grabar, "Trônes épiscopaux du XIème et XIIème siècle" in vol. 16 (1954) of the Wallraf-Richartz *Jahrbuch* (Verlag E. A. Seemann, Köln). I owe this reference to Professor Ilene Forsyth of the University of Michigan.

13. Dimitri Tselos has shown that Kröger was also indebted to Richardson in his project of 1900–1902 for the St. Jacob church in Dresden in "Richardson's Influence on European Architecture," *Journal of the Society of Architectural Historians* 29 (1970): 156–162. Tselos, I think, understates the difficulty of distinguishing Richardsonian work from the native German Romanesque revival.

14. Alan Gowans, *Images of American Living* (Philadelphia and New York, 1964), p. 350.

15. Vogel is not included in the 1910 edition of *Wer Ist's?* or in any similar compilation that I have been able to consult. He is apparently a rather shadowy character.

Among all the European architects who came to the United States prior to the First World War, Adolf Loos (1870–1933) is the most mysterious. While we have a good deal of documentation on the travels of men like Berlage and C. H. Reilly, there is no record of the journey of Loos other than the scanty references in his own writings. This is astonishing, when one considers the stature of the man in the Modern Movement and the amount that has been written about him. He stayed three years in this country (1893–1896) visiting New York, Philadelphia, Chicago, and St. Louis, and yet he is almost impossible to trace. Perhaps Nikolaus Pevsner has got at the heart of the problem when he calls Loos "an enigma." He seems to have been one of those men who instinctively covered his tracks (Figure 62).

When Loos came to the United States, he was twenty-three years old. The son of a stonemason and sculptor at Brno in Moravia, at that time an Austrian province, he had received his grammar school education from the Benedictines at the famous monastery of Melk, taken technical training at Liberec (Reichenberg), Bohemia, and in Dresden, and done his military service as a one-year volunteer. His trip to the New World was apparently the occasion of a tremendous family fight. Loos always got along badly with his mother, and his third wife indicates that they had a terrible struggle. Finally, however, his mother agreed to pay his passage, and he set off to visit the Chicago World's Fair, which he was to discuss in one of his first essays. His motives, says Frau Elsie Altmann Loos, were simply those of any adventurous young man in Central Europe in the 1890s. He felt oppressed by the illiberal atmosphere and the official culture of the Austro-Hungarian Empire. In retrospect this culture does not seem to have been anywhere near so oppressive as it then appeared, but it certainly looked stuffy to progressive spirits in the nineties. America, in contrast, looked like the land of opportunity, where anything was possible.[1]

It is also well to note that in the early nineties at least one

Figure 62
Adolf Loos about 1910

important recent American building had received favorable publicity in Vienna. This was the Auditorium Hotel and Opera House of Adler and Sullivan (1886–1889), which had been published in the *Wochenschrift* of the Austrian Architectural and Engineering Society for March 28, 1890. The article included elevations, plans, and sections of this great structure, and particular attention was paid to problems of acoustics and to the complicated stage machinery. The reason for this interest is easy to perceive. Vienna has traditionally been one of the great European centers for opera production, and the Viennese would have naturally been intrigued with the manner in which Dankmar Adler had solved the complicated technical problems associated with this type of building. Then, too, there is an element of local interest here. Adler had made a trip to Europe to examine the latest improvements in stage design, and he had been particularly impressed by the opera houses at Halle and Budapest, which used machinery designed and built by the Asphaleia Gesellschaft of Vienna. These theaters employed hydraulic apparatus to elevate and depress the stage floor, and Adler asked the company to make designs for similar machinery for the Auditorium. Ultimately there were so many divergencies between American and Austrian engineering practices that Paul Mueller in Chicago had to redraw the Asphaleia plans, but the Viennese could still take pride in American use of principles developed by one of their firms. Loos, who had a lively interest in technology of all kinds, and was also something of an opera fan, might very well have wanted to see this edifice. In addition, he had an uncle in Philadelphia who was a watch repairman on Chestnut Street, and this individual was apparently able to help him out during his first few months in America. It was, then, a perfectly natural thing for him to spend his *Wanderjahr* in the United States.

Unlike Hendrik Berlage and Charles H. Reilly, Loos came to the United States knowing very little English and without any professional reputation or position. As a consequence, he

saw a side of American life of which they were quite igno-
rant. Probably because of his linguistic deficiency and lack
of professional connections, Loos was never able to secure
work in an American architectural office. Instead, he washed
dishes, laid floors, and for a while even worked as a music
critic. This last adventure took place in Manhattan, and Loos
used it in one of the wryly humorous anecdotes about himself which are scattered through his two volumes of essays,
Ins Leere gesprochen (1921) and *Trotzdem* (1930). Apparently he was working as a reporter for a German language
newspaper at the time, and the assignment to review a performance of *Carmen* at the Metropolitan Opera came to him because the paper's regular music critic had unexpectedly gone
over to the English language press. According to his own account, he carried it through with great aplomb, and in his
essay uses the episode to make the point that it is easy to
become an expert on anything if one is willing to acquire the
proper jargon. The details of the story suggest that it was
probably in the substantial German communities of the great
American cities that Loos moved rather than in the architectural world, which tended in those years to be dominated by
men of English descent. There were, of course, a few German-
speaking architects in most of the major cities (one thinks
immediately of Leopold Eidlitz in New York and Dankmar
Adler in Chicago) but Loos evidently failed to make contact
with them. If he had done so, his stay in the United States
might have been much easier. In his autobiography Richard
Neutra, who knew Loos well, recalled that he loved to tell of
his experiences in America but always stressed his extreme
poverty while in the country. Despite the fact that his years
here had been difficult, Loos evidently retained a deep affec-
tion for the United States.[2]

What was the effect upon the young Loos of his prolonged
sojourn in America? It came at a time that is usually extremely important for the formation of an architect: the years

between the completion of his formal education and his actual engagement in practice. The question is hard to answer because of the paucity of clues in Loos's writings and the way in which he distorted his experience. The music critic episode, for example, supposedly occurred in 1895 when he was working for the *New Yorker Bannerträger.* There was, in fact, no such paper in New York at that date. There was, however, a German weekly called *Das National Banner,* and there is no reason to suppose that Loos did not write for it. The entire story is in keeping with his character. The de Reszke brothers, Emma Calvé, and Nellie Melba were, indeed, starring in one of the Metropolitan's most famous productions of *Carmen* in that year, and it was this cast that Loos must have heard. In short, there is no reason to doubt the general accuracy of the story, but some of the details are questionable. Loos was one of those men who love to make myths about themselves, and this is a good example.

American influence on the work of Loos operates on two levels: the practical and the theoretical. The first category is the less important. Loos's first independent jobs in Vienna, which date from the late 1890s, included a large number of apartment remodelings. This was to be expected, since most Viennese were apartment dwellers; only a relatively small proportion could afford the luxury of a detached house. In these remodelings Loos used certain features derived from the architecture of H. H. Richardson. In 1930 Richard Neutra, a student of Loos and a man who knew American architecture well, noted particularly his employment of false beams in light oak put in for show and fireplaces in exposed brickwork. He added, "But apart from such superficialities, it is the first time that a creative, gifted European has adopted effective features from the American style and has used them as points of departure for his own schemes."[3] Neutra was evidently unaware of the earlier Richardsonian work in Scandinavia. Loos might, of course, have seen the interiors of the MacVeagh and Glessner houses in Chicago, and perhaps also the Potter house in St. Louis, all of which were done in the years 1885–1887. *Neubauten in Nordamerika,* the important publication of 1897 by Graef and Hinckeldeyn, is also a possibility. The interior of the H. D. Yerxa house, built in Cambridge, Massachusetts, in 1894 by Hartwell and Richardson (Figure 63), is the type of work that might have appealed to him. It is a scaled-down version of H. H. Richardson's hall for the John Hay house of 1884–1886 in Washington, D.C. (Figure 64). We are inclined to think, however, that Loos must actually have visited one or two interiors by Richardson himself during his American sojourn. His handling of the Richardsonian elements is too assured to have been gained merely from books. The Glessner house in Chicago, built in 1885–1887, is perhaps the most likely possibility (Figures 65 and 66).

For the first ten years of his practice Loos was much concerned with the motifs of the chimney corner and the beamed ceiling. A crayon sketch of ca. 1899 is particularly interesting because it is a fantasy design and presumably an ideal solution to the problem of uniting fireplace recess and interior space (Figure 67); also, it is worked out in much greater detail than most drawings by Loos (some of his best sketches are on the backs of wine cards and menus). Ludwig Münz and Gustav Künstler observe that Loos knew from the beginning that the combination could be solved only architecturally:

In a room which has a long outside wall with two rows of charming blue and yellow windows, the fireplace recess has been organically built in between the entrance door on the left and the staircase to a gallery; the bend in the stairs makes the fireplace recess considerably lower than the rest of the hall.[4]

The idea of the fireplace niche occurs again in a pencil sketch, also of ca. 1899 (Figure 68); apparently the problem was of real concern to Loos. It is interesting to note that a number of such niches were published in the 1897 edition of *Neubauten.* The inglenooks at the Chisholm house in Cleveland of 1888 by Charles F. Schweinfurth and at the A. Moore

Figure 64
H. H. Richardson, interior
John Hay house,
Washington, D.C., 1884–
1886

Figure 65
H. H. Richardson, interior,
Glessner house, Chicago,
Illinois, 1885–1887

Figure 66
H. H. Richardson, dining
room, Glessner house,
Chicago, Illinois, 1885–1887

Figure 67
Adolf Loos, crayon sketch,
ca. 1899

Figure 68
Adolf Loos, pencil sketch,
ca. 1899.

Figure 69
Charles F. Schweinfurth,
Chisholm house, Cleveland,
Ohio, 1888. Plate from
Neubauten in Nordamerika,
Berlin, 1905

Figure 70
Marble and Larsen, A.
Moore House, Chicago,
Illinois, 1894. Plate from
Neubauten in Nordamerika,
Berlin, 1905

Figure 71
Adolf Loos apartment,
Vienna, 1903

Figure 72
Treat and Foltz, fireplace,
Martin Ryerson house,
Chicago, Illinois, 1886–
1887. Plate from *Neubauten
in Nordamerika,* Berlin,
1905

Figure 73
Adolf Loos, Leopold Langer
apartment, Vienna, 1901

house on Michigan Avenue in Chicago of 1894 by Marble and Larsen are typical (Figures 69 and 70). Loos might also have been affected by these illustrations.

In the architect's executed work the union of interior space and fireplace niche is best seen in his own apartment, which is today preserved in the Museum of the City of Vienna (Figure 71). Here the inglenook idea is simplified and dramatized, and all the florid decoration that is so characteristic of the American examples is removed. For a fireplace hood, Loos uses a form that is somewhat like that in the Martin Ryerson house in Chicago of 1886–1887 (Figure 72) but fashions it entirely of metal with no foliate adornment whatever. Most important of all is the change in scale. In the American examples the spatial design is lavish, and despite the nature of the problem, almost grandiose. Loos, on the other hand, was a true Viennese, and his imagination worked particularly well in a tight and intricate way. One sometimes has the feeling that he might have been a great jewelry designer. A similar approach to the problem of the fireplace niche can be seen in the Leopold Langer apartment of 1901 (Figure 73). Especially noteworthy in these interiors is an element of simplicity that would have appeared quite revolutionary in comparison with the ordinary Viennese living room of the day, and this, too, may derive from Richardson. Munz and Künstler remark:

Two things must not be overlooked: compared with middle class homes of the time in Europe, either paying homage to the Renaissance or else to the Sezession, Richardson's interiors are of classic simplicity; and also the combination of high and low spaces serves the needs of living, work and social intercourse in the room while affording seclusion in the fireplace recess hard by.[5]

In short, American interiors were important to Loos in the first few years of his practice. He could have known them either through personal experience or through publications.

In this decade the architect's mature treatment of interiors

began to emerge, and it should be noted that it had very little
to do either with American precedent or with the international style of the 1920s, with which he is too frequently associated. The typical Loosian handling of interior surfaces is
well represented in the flat for Rudolf Kraus of 1907 (Figure
74). In these dwellings the emphasis is on extremely rich textures, usually composed so as to bring out the veining of the
marble that he loved to employ. The mature work of Loos
probably owes more to his background as a stonemason than
to any other single factor. He also used a great many rich
woods, particularly mahogany, and there is a continual interest in spatial illusionism, as in the Kärtner Bar of 1907
(Figures 75, 76, and 77); as the photographs reveal, much of
the powerful effect of this tiny interior is due to the use of
mirrors. Also noteworthy is the cramped and twisting quality
of the staircase; again one is reminded of a bit of intricate
jewelry. The treatment is almost diametrically opposed to the
ample handling of the stairs in the Richardsonian Yerxa
house. In his late work he occasionally returned to the motif
of the fireplace niche in projects where it fitted into the program, as in the Villa Khuner of 1930 at Semmering (Figure
78). In part, this highly characteristic personal style was a
reaction against the excesses of the Viennese Sezession
movement. It had also, however, an extremely puritanical
element that was all his own. His most important work, the
business building on the Michaelerplatz for Leopold Gold-
man of 1910 (Figure 79), could never be mistaken for an
American commercial structure of the period. This edifice,
which today appears to be not only fine architecture but also
a distinguished bit of urbanism, caused an immense uproar
in the Vienna of 1910. Its construction was actually inter-
rupted by official intervention as a consequence of public
opinion, and Loos suffered a serious case of nervous stom-
ach because of the aggravation that he had to endure. The
charming and sensitive Ilse Barea, who was a girl of eleven at
the time when the structure was going up, recalls that she

was ". . . as childishly incensed as any grown-up philistine that he dared put it next to the Hofburg and the old Michaelerhaus. What especially annoyed me was the idea that it had no moulding or scroll in which the snow could settle in the gentle lines I loved."[6] Both the writings and the architecture of Loos were extremely controversial.

As Nikolaus Pevsner has pointed out, the polemical journalism of Loos had two objectives. On the one hand, he fought hard against historicism, which in the late nineteenth century was perhaps more strongly entrenched in Vienna than anywhere else in Europe. In painting, the seventies and eighties had been dominated by the grand historical style of Makart, whose enormous canvases celebrated the past glories of the Austro-Hungarian empire. In architecture it was the period of the huge neobaroque edifices on the Ringstrasse, most of them commissioned by the imperial government. The unyielding hostility of the administration of Franz Josef to anything new in the visual arts needs to be stressed. The anecdote concerning the archduke Franz Ferdinand's reaction to the paintings of Oskar Kokoschka is typical; on seeing them in 1911 he remarked, "The fellow ought to have every bone in his body broken." Not so well known but more important for architecture is the story of the archduke's visit to the church of the Steinhof Mental Hospital in the company of Otto Wagner, who escorted him through the newly completed edifice (Figure 80). The archduke showed his dislike of the structure by remarking that the old style (the baroque of Maria Theresa) was still the best. The architect, who knew the interest of his royal highness in military affairs, pointed out that the empire would hesitate to use cannon from that period in its armies, but this argument failed to impress the heir to the throne. With unaccustomed asperity Wagner concluded that whatever may have been its political consequences, the assassination of Franz Ferdinand was the greatest boon that had ever been conferred upon modern architecture in Austria.

Figure 74
Adolf Loos, Rudolf Kraus
apartment, Vienna, 1907

Figure 75
Adolf Loos, Kärtner Bar,
Vienna, 1907

Figure 76
Adolf Loos, Kärtner Bar,
Vienna, 1907

Figure 77
Adolf Loos, Kärtner Bar,
staircase, Vienna, 1907

Figure 78
Adolf Loos, Villa Khuner,
Semmering, 1930

Figure 79
Adolf Loos, Goldman-
Salatsch Store, Vienna,
1910

Figure 80
Otto Wagner, Kirche am
Steinhof, Vienna, 1907–
1908

While Loos fought hard against the adamant historicism represented by the imperial court, he also fought with equal vigor against the decorative style espoused by the Sezession architects and their contemporaries in the Art Nouveau movement. In 1897 he was dubious about Liberty's in London, Bing's shop in Paris, and the exhibition of Dresden; a year later he criticized a similar show of the new work in Munich. His most biting language was probably reserved for van de Velde, but he was almost equally hard on Hofmann and Olbrich. Concerning van de Velde he wrote, "I tell you that the time will come when the furnishing of a prison cell by Professor van de Velde will be considered aggravation of the sentence."[7] Of the tableware designed by Olbrich he said, "Cutlery for people who can eat, after the English fashion, and who cannot eat, from designs by Olbrich." Frequently Loos made his points by means of anecdotes and parables. Perhaps the most forceful of these is the story of the saddlemaker, which has been translated by Nikolaus Pevsner:

Once upon a time there was a saddle-maker, a competent good craftsman. He made saddles quite different in form from those of past centuries or from Turkish or Japanese saddles. That is, he made modern saddles. But that he did not know. He only knew that he made saddles, as well as he could. Then in his town a strange movement arrived. It was called *Sezession.* It demanded that only modern things for everyday use should be made. When the saddle-maker heard this, he took one of his best saddles and went to one of the leaders of the Sezession. "Professor," he said, for the leaders had at once been made professors, "I have heard of your demands. I too am a modern person. I would like to work modern. Tell me: is this saddle modern?" The professor looked at the saddle and then delivered a long lecture in which the terms art in the crafts, individuality, modern, Hermann Bahr, Ruskin, applied art, appeared time and again. The result was: "No—this is not a modern saddle." Deeply mortified the saddle-maker went away. He thought, worked and thought again. But however hard he tried to comply with the professor's demands, he would in the end be back at his old saddle. So he went sadly back to the professor who said: "My dear man, you have no imagination." Yes, that was it. No imagination. But he had not realized that

that was needed for saddle-making. Had he had it, he would
surely have become a painter or a sculptor, or a poet, or a
composer. But the professor said: "Come back tomorrow.
It is our job to promote trades and fertilize them with new
ideas. I'll see what I can do." And in his studio at the art
school he announced as a programme: Design for a saddle.
The next day the saddle-maker returned. The professor could
show him forty-nine designs. He had only forty-four students,
but five he had done himself. They were meant to go into
The Studio, because there was a certain mood in them. The
saddle-maker looked long at the drawings, and his eyes grew
ever more serene. Then he said: "Professor, if I knew as
little of horses, of horsemanship, of leather and workman-
ship as you do, I would have your imagination." And now he
lives happy and contented and makes saddles. Are they
modern? He does not know. They are saddles.[8]

The story is, of course, a pointed comment on the simplification that all types of industrial design necessarily had
to undergo in the late nineteenth century. It was in the
understanding of this simplification that his American experience helped Loos.

In this connection it is well to observe that the writings
of Loos reveal a mind that was interested in all aspects of
design. His first publications in *Die neue freie Presse* were
reviews of the industrial arts section at the Vienna Exhibition
of 1898, which was held to celebrate the fiftieth anniversary
of the coronation of Franz Josef. The paper for which he was
writing was the largest, most influential daily in the Austro-
Hungarian empire. Its editor, the formidable Israel Zangwill
(one of the founders of modern Zionism) was one of the important personages of Vienna. That the young, unknown Loos
was able to achieve publication in this prestigious journal
is evidence of Zangwill's astuteness. Part of the impact of
these pieces comes from their style. Instead of the customary
convoluted grammatical structure of that day, Loos used
short sentences and biting phrases; furthermore he displayed
a great deal of wit, a quality always dear to the hearts of the
Viennese. He also employed a number of colloquialisms,
which are, unhappily, almost impossible to translate. The
critic Ludwig Hevesi, one of the defenders of the Sezession

movement, commented on Loos's Americanism and on his style: "Loos comes from America and has announced this fact in a series of sharp and biting artistic criticisms. For him Brother Jonathan is the most modern of the moderns."[9]

His essays, then, dealt with problems of style in clothing and articles of everyday use: shoes, furniture, hardware, and the like. In all these matters he found Viennese taste extremely backward, and as the remark about Olbrich's cutlery indicates, generally held up English products as models. He was obviously an admirer of William Morris and of the Arts and Crafts Movement. It was this line of thought that led him to his well-known panegyric on "The Plumber" and ultimately to his even more famous essay on "Ornament and Crime." In these works Loos moved from an analysis of common household objects to conclusions that affected the entire history of the Modern Movement. At the same time most of his writing has a characteristic Viennese ambiance. It cannot be understood without many references to the Viennese scene of his day. Indeed, in certain respects he was merely voicing rather widespread Viennese attitudes of the period. There is, for example, nothing very remarkable about his admiration for the English. It was a fairly common upper-middle-class attitude. In Heimito von Doderer's excellent novel *The Waterfalls of Slunj* the author notes that his two antiheroes, Robert and Donald Clayton, have little difficulty in gaining entree into Viennese upper-middle-class society. They are actually helped by the fact that they are English. Von Doderer writes:

. . . for at that period the taste for English style was well on its way to permeating the whole Continent in a multitude of little streams, entering all forms of life. Even in the previous century that shrewd spirit the dramatist Johann Nestroy had made fun of the Anglomaniacs; and around 1900, as much later still, it was the normal thing to keep a tennis score in English, as well as using the English terms in cricket and football.[10]

The position of Loos was probably not so isolated as his partisans would have us believe. In the 1920s another Loos,

Anita, remarked that there was no language barrier to sur-
mount in Vienna; the people had always been anglophiles,
and it was chic to speak English.[11]

While the majority of Loos's examples of good and sensible
living were English, a substantial number were American,
and in certain very important respects his vision of the future
for twentieth-century man was heavily influenced by his stay
in the United States. For him, the American was one who
had discarded the outmoded cultural equipment of the
nineteenth century and had a direct and sensible attitude
toward life. From 1893 to 1896 Loos spent most of his time
among immigrants, and he observed that they had generally
put behind them the bitter national rivalries of the Old World.
Concerning this experience Richard Neutra wrote:

To him America was the land of unshackled minds—of
people with debunked minds, let us say—of people brought
close to life's realities . . . realities in a new time, naively,
subconsciously kept in matter-of-fact working order. People
here, as he saw them, had reverted to a sound attitude which
had been lost in the old country. At the same time they had
golden hearts compared to the pettier or more sophisticated
quarrelers back home.[12]

It is not surprising that Loos was a student of Walt Whitman
and often quoted him in conversation. The 1898 essay on
"The Shoemaker" contains two stanzas of "Pioneers! O
Pioneers!" in an excellent German translation. It might be
said that Loos thought of himself as a pioneer in Whitman's
sense of the word and of his architecture as a suitable kind
of building for men and women who shared his general
feeling about life.

Up to this point Loos, as Nikolaus Pevsner has pointed out,
sounds very much like Louis Sullivan, who in 1892 had published an article arguing that it would be a good thing if architects refrained from designing ornament altogether for a
period of years so that they could concentrate on the production of buildings "well formed and comely in the nude."
There is, however, little likelihood that Loos was familiar with

this article, which appeared in a rather obscure publication. In view of Loos's lack of knowledge of English in 1893 and Sullivan's aristocratic aloofness, there is also very little possibility that the two men made personal contact. Loos must, of course, have seen a good many Adler and Sullivan edifices in Chicago. He could hardly have missed the Transportation Building at the Fair, but, considering his own predilections for plain surfaces and his denial of ornament, it is questionable that he would have been enthusiastic about the famous Golden Door. As we have seen, the architect who appealed to him was Richardson. The only American artist whom he mentions in his 1898 reviews for *Die neue freie Presse* was the graphic designer Will Bradley; about him Loos had many good things to say.

It should also be emphasized that Loos and Sullivan were entirely different types of writer. Sullivan thought of himself as a philosopher and poet, whose inspirational message would call his fellow citizens from their materialistic ways. During his lifetime he was never read by more than a handful of followers. Loos, on the other hand, wrote for the biggest and most authoritative daily newspaper in Vienna. He, too, was a man with a message, but it was much more down-to-earth. He achieved a great public impact because he delivered it in the witty manner traditional in Viennese journalism. It was obviously quite possible for Chicago to ignore Sullivan—indeed, a peculiar masochistic element in his personality seems to have demanded this treatment—but in Vienna nobody could ignore Loos. His criticisms were simply too well put to be shaken off easily. It is suggestive that Karl Kraus, one of the most powerful of Viennese journalists, was a close friend of Loos, and that the two worked together in 1918 on plans for a ministry of art in the new Austrian republic. In 1920–1922 Loos was chief architect in the Viennese Department of Housing. This was a kind of public appointment that was always denied to Sullivan.

An additional point of difference between the theories of

Sullivan and Loos is to be found in their attitudes toward classicism. In 1910 Loos wrote: "On the threshold of the nineteenth century stood Schinkel. May light from this towering figure fall on the coming generation of our architects,"[13] and in 1924 he expressed approval of the rebirth of classicism in France in what was presumably a reference to Perret. Perhaps because of his training at the Ecole des Beaux-Arts at a time (1874–1876) when that institution preached a decadent classicism, Sullivan was always adamant in his opposition to this doctrine in all its forms. Every type of classicism seemed to him to be too far removed from the realities of contemporary culture to provide effective architectural solutions to the major building problems of the day. Despite his seeming radicalism, Loos was, in fact, the most traditionally minded among the pioneers of the Modern Movement. As Richard Neutra has indicated, he reached out for some kind of contact with history in order to produce a quality of "lastingness" and thus escape the ephemeral fashions of his period.[14]

It would appear, then, that there was indeed an American element in the work of Adolf Loos, but it is important not to overstate the case. In certain ways Richardson's interiors were influential in his early work, and his experience of American life helped to shape the intellectual background that he brought to his writings. There is, however, very little evidence that Louis Sullivan was significant to him in any substantial degree.

Notes

1. Elsie Altmann Loos, *Adolf Loos, der Mensch* (Vienna and Munich, 1968), pp. 18–22. This book, by Loos's third wife, who divorced him in 1928, must obviously be used with caution. The last years of their marriage were characterized by extreme bitterness. I am, however, inclined to accept her account of conversations with Loos in 1917–1918, at the time when he was courting her.

2. The records of Loos's schooling in Austria show no evidence of any study of the English language, and it is highly unlikely that *at this time* he spoke it at all. In later years he made several trips to

England and enjoyed speaking the language with his second wife, who was a Scotch chorus girl. Neutra's account of Loos's American reminiscences is contained in an autobiographical volume, *Life and Shape* (New York, 1962), pp. 160–170.

3. Richard Neutra, *Neues Bauen in der Welt,* vol. 2: *Amerika* (Vienna, 1930), p. 44.

4. Ludwig Münz and Gustav Künstler, *Adolf Loos: Pioneer of Modern Architecture,* trans. Harold Meek (New York and Washington, 1966), p. 59.

5. Ibid. In this connection I would like to note that while this book was in press, Professor Stefan Muthesius of the University of Norwich very kindly called my attention to a review of *Neubauten in Nordamerika* by Richard Streiter in his *Architektonische Stilfragen* (Berlin, 1898). Streiter, a prominent art historian and critic, had some reservations about the influence of Richardson but was extremely enthusiastic about the interiors shown by Graef and Hinckeldeyn. They were, in his opinion, well adapted to all the requirements of contemporary living, and he particularly admired the skill of the American architects in handling woodwork and fireplaces.

6. Ilse Barea, *Vienna: Legend and Reality* (London, 1966), p. 109.

7. Adolf Loos, *Sämtliche Schriften* (Vienna and Munich, 1962), p. 288.

8. Nikolaus Pevsner, quoted in Münz and Künstler, *Adolf Loos,* pp. 16–17.

9. Hevesi is quoted in Sokratis Dimitriou, "Adolf Loos: Gedanken zum Ursprung von Lehre und Werk," *Bauforum* 21 (December 1970): 22.

10. Heimito von Doderer, *The Waterfalls of Slunj,* trans. Eithne Wilkins and Ernst Karser (New York, 1967), pp. 138–139.

11. Anita Loos, *A Girl Like I* (New York, 1966), p. 241.

12. Richard Neutra, *Life and Shape* (New York, 1962), p. 162.

13. Loos, *Sämtliche Schriften,* p. 318.

14. Roland L. Schachel, in "Adolf Loos, Amerika und die Antike," *Alte und moderne Kunst,* no. 113 (November–December 1970), pp. 6–10, argues that much of Loos's classicism derives from his American experience. I find myself unable to accept this contention. Schinkel is a far likelier source. See also Richard Neutra's review of Münz and Künstler, *Adolf Loos,* in *Architectural Forum* 123 (August 1966): 89.

In Sweden and Denmark the architectural situation in the late nineteenth century was, as elsewhere in Europe, confused. The distinguished Swedish art historian Johnny Roosval called the main tendency of the period "eclectic romanticism" and noted that the movement used the palaces of the early Italian Renaissance in Venice and Florence as models. A good many examples of this style can be found in Stockholm, and very often they will remind an American observer of the New York town houses of McKim, Mead & White. They are spacious structures with all details well adapted in form and scale to aristocratic city living.

To this kind of design Roosval, writing in 1932, contrasted two tendencies that he labeled "National Romanticism" and "Naturalism." The first of these lines of development is today much the better known. Its chief monument is the famous Stockholm City Hall by Ragnar Östberg (1905–1923). This edifice (Figure 81) was, as G. E. Kidder Smith remarks, " . . . the first really important piece of architecture in Sweden in two hundred years."[1] For the tourist, even today it is perhaps the single best-known building in the city. In the long run, however, the movement that Roosval called naturalism was to be more important. It is suggestive that he felt it was " . . . partly dependent on influence from the American Middle West."[2] Roosval was probably the first art historian to comment on the importance of H. H. Richardson for Swedish architects in the 1890s.

In Sweden serious interest in American architecture seems to have begun in the 1880s. The key figure in the story is Johan Henrik Palme, a civil servant and citizen of Stockholm who became distressed over the disorderly growth of the city. Born in Kalmar in 1841, Palme moved to Stockholm in 1872 and from 1876 onward was a town councillor of the Swedish capital. The 1870s witnessed the building of many large and ugly apartment blocks in the city, and Palme, like many civic-minded men of that day, began to search about for an alternative. In 1888 he took an extended trip to the

Figure 81
Ragnar Östberg, Stockholm
City Hall, 1905–1923

Figure 82
H. H. Richardson, Stoughton
house, Cambridge,
Massachusetts, 1880–1881

Figure 83
Swedish house at
Saltsjöbaden, ca. 1890

Figure 84
Swedish house at
Saltsjobaden, ca. 1890

United States to look at garden suburbs around Philadelphia, New York, San Francisco, and Chicago. Among those that he visited were Yonkers and, in all probability, Riverside, the outstanding achievement of Frederick Law Olmsted. Palme was impressed by the fact that the purchase of a large block of land by an individual or a group permitted a unified development and savings on the installation of utilities. On his return to Stockholm he found that Baron Montgomery-Cedarhelm, a nobleman who owned a substantial tract of land north of the city, was willing to sell. The name of the area was Djursholm, and with three associates Palme formed a company and purchased it for 500,000 kroner on June 8, 1889. Subsequently he devoted a great deal of time to the development of Djursholm.[3] Today it has a startling resemblance to its American prototypes both in planning and in the houses that were built there. Much the same thing can be said about Saltsjöbaden, another garden suburb developed by the famous Wallenberg family in the 1890s. Many of the dwellings in these Stockholm suburbs of the late nineteenth century are Swedish versions of the shingle style, so popular in American resort areas at the same period. Of this genre Richardson's well-known Stoughton house at Cambridge, Massachusetts (Figure 82), is probably the best-known example. By comparison a Swedish house at Saltsjöbaden (Figures 83 and 84) looks rather clumsy. The shingles are, of course, an old tradition in this part of the world, but the round tower is decidedly Richardsonian.

While the shingled houses in Djursholm and Saltsjöbaden are certainly noteworthy, Richardson's influence in Scandinavia was not limited to the domestic field or to any one circle of architects. In various ways he affected almost the entire generation of architects who came to maturity around 1890. The case of Isak G. Clason (1856–1930) is particularly interesting. Clason, perhaps the central figure of this group, never really got away from historicism but was nevertheless a very solid type of designer. In his most important work Rich-

ardson is mixed with Norman Shaw. A recent biography remarks:

> About 1890 Clason, in common with his colleagues, was
> also subject to impulses from the American architect H. H.
> Richardson and his school, though at first only in the form
> of periodicals and commercial collections of photographs.
> Typical of Clason's architecture of this period is the direct
> and effortless expression of the spatial content of the
> building in its external form, with the development of vari-
> able fenestration. Added to this is a peculiar concept of
> materials. Stone, brick, and wood are used not merely as
> media for form but equally for the sake of their own struc-
> ture. In the building as a whole the material has the role of
> organic embodiment intimately related to the other media of
> expressions. This concept originates with Norman Shaw and
> H. H. Richardson.[4]

Another Richardsonian architect was Hans Hedlund (1855–
1931), who practiced mostly in Göteborg, a city always
known for its Atlantic orientation. A graduate of the Chalmers
Institute of Technology and the Academy of Art in Stockholm, he worked in Göteborg from 1881 onward, in later
years in collaboration with his son, Bjarner. Hedlund was especially well known for his libraries, a building type in which
the American master excelled. His Dickson Library of 1895
(Figure 85) and City Library of 1898 (Figure 86) are exceedingly Richardsonian.

More articulate than either Clason or Hedlund was Ferdinand Boberg, who was born in 1860 into an old Swedish
family long connected with the famous copper mines at
Falun. Of an extremely romantic temperament, Boberg displayed an extraordinary interest in the world outside Sweden
from the days of his youth. A recent book, *Bobergiana*
(Stockholm, 1958), lists a remarkable series of 120 long
foreign trips extending over a period of fifty-four years and
including journeys to Africa, India, East Asia, and the United
States. Well-connected with the Swedish aristocracy, he often
traveled in the company of the then crown prince and prin-
cess. These journeys gave him a thoroughly international attitude, and his many connections with professional people
in Western Europe convinced him that internationalism was

the only hope for Swedish culture, which seemed to him generally narrow and parochial. At this point it is well to observe that Sweden, like Denmark, experienced a rather disappointing nineteenth century. The country yielded its last Continental possessions in the Napoleonic wars, and in the middle and latter years of the century it lost hundreds of thousands of its most productive citizens to the United States through emigration. Vilhelm Moberg's superb trilogy, *Unto a Good Land* (New York, 1954), gives a fine description of the depressed agricultural economy that produced this remarkable mass movement. Until about 1900 Sweden did not share in the rapid economic progress of France, Britain, and Germany, and it was often ranked as one of the least prosperous nations in Europe. In the light of these conditions it is not surprising that the young Boberg turned outward.

Where Boberg first ran across H. H. Richardson is not entirely clear. It may well have been in one of the English or German publications of Richardson's work that appeared in the 1880s. His first Richardsonian building was the Fire Station for Gavle, an industrial city about one hundred miles north of Stockholm. Designed and built in 1890, it was done in a tawny yellow brick rather than the rough masonry that is usually associated with Richardson (Figures 87 and 88). With its powerful conical towers and rhythmical window groupings, it might almost be from the office of the master himself. Widely admired in Sweden, it was also published in the English journal, *Academy Architecture,* which, until 1910 or so, showed a remarkable hospitality to the new style developing in Europe and America.

Boberg's next important structure was the Stockholm Electric Works of 1892 (Figures 89 and 90). With its powerful arched entryway and rugged ashlar, this structure created a sensation in the city; indicative of Boberg's effort at modernity was the frieze of electric light bulbs, which replaced the egg-and-dart or bead-and-reel molding usually employed in this situation. The Electric Works was accompanied by two other Richardsonian buildings, the Workmen's Institute

Figure 85
Hans Hedlund, Dickson
Library, Göteborg, Sweden,
1895

Figure 86
Hans Hedlund, City Library,
Göteborg, Sweden, 1898

Figure 87
Ferdinand Boberg, Fire Station, Gavle, Sweden, 1890

Figure 88
Ferdinand Boberg, Fire
Station, Gavle, Sweden,
entry way, 1890

Figure 89
Ferdinand Boberg, Electric
Works, Stockholm, 1892

Figure 90
Ferdinand Boberg, Electric
Works, Stockholm, detail of
entrance, 1892

Figure 91
Carl Möller, Workman's
Institute, Stockholm,
1893–1894

Figure 92
Ludvig Peterson, Högonäs
Store, Stockholm, 1889–
1891

Figure 93
H. H. Richardson, Winn
Library, Woburn,
Massachusetts, 1877

by Carl Moller of 1893–1894 (Figure 91) and the Högonäs
Store by Ludvig Peterson of 1889–1891 (Figure 92). Like the
Electric Works, both were powerful masonry structures with
characteristic Richardsonian window groupings. Although
all of these edifices have unhappily been destroyed, a few
traces of the Swedish Richardsonian can still be seen in
various apartments scattered throughout the city. Stockholm's American inheritance is thus barely visible.

Boberg himself made a trip to the United States in 1893 in
connection with the Swedish Pavilion at the Chicago World's
Fair, and while in this country he evidently tried to see as
much of the new architecture as possible. It is interesting to
note that although he actually worked in the office of Adler
and Sullivan for a few months, it was the Richardsonian
style that appealed to him. In Chicago he might, of course,
have seen two of Richardson's greatest works, the Glessner
House and the Marshall Field Wholesale Store, both done in
1885–1887. There were, in fact, about twenty Swedish architects who visited the United States in connection with the
Fair. It is of considerable importance as the first major American showing of Swedish arts and crafts. One also wonders if
the success of Anders Zorn's pictures in Charles Atwood's
Fine Arts Building did not have a lot to do with that artist's
phenomenal popularity in Chicago.[5]

Boberg thought his American experience was of sufficient
interest to his Swedish colleagues to write two articles
based on it for *Teknisk tidskrift* in 1896. In these pieces, for
a magazine that was the ancestor of the present *Arkitektur,*
he dealt with "Public Libraries in the United States." The
second article illustrated Richardson's Winn Library at Woburn, Massachusetts (Figure 93). While Boberg did not like
the combination of local museum and library here (the result
of a large private donation) he was full of admiration for
Richardson's handling of the problems of circulation and
book storage. He was also enormously impressed with the
development of the public library movement in the United

States. We sometimes forget that the modern public library is essentially an American invention, and Richardson's serious treatment of this novel institution evidently came as a shock to Boberg. In addition, he was impressed with Richardson's architecture as an attempt to get away from the stylistic merry-go-round of the nineteenth century and to return to fundamentals.

Boberg's career after 1900 is instructive. Having begun as the representative of international modernism, he became increasingly superficial after the turn of the century. At the Stockholm Exhibition in 1909 he was severely criticized by Ivar Tengbom, one of the leaders of the new generation, for his indifference to the nature of materials. The difficulty seems to have been that Boberg was working more and more for the high aristocracy and developing into a designer of ornament. His project for the Nobel Foundation building of 1911 came in for even heavier criticism from Ragnar Östberg. He retired from active practice in 1915 and devoted the last fifteen years of his life to traveling about Sweden by automobile (an ancient Volvo) and recording old buildings in thousands of charcoal drawings that are now preserved in Swedish museums. Since many of these structures were in ruinous condition, Boberg performed a useful task. One must. observe, however, that he had failed to move with the times and that his excellent social connections had far too much effect upon the configuration of his career.

George A. Nilsson (1871–1949) was a far more conventional personality than Boberg, and his achievement was very different in character. Although he was highly esteemed in his own lifetime, he disliked publicity, and the young Swedish architectural critic Bjorn Linn has aptly described him as "the Quiet Revolutionary."[6] Most of his life was concerned with the problem of modernizing Swedish school design, and in this area he accomplished an important but unspectacular job. His position in this field may be compared with that of Lawrence Perkins in the United States. He also, however, did two business buildings in Stockholm, and in these he showed complete awareness of the most advanced principles of contemporary architectural design. The larger, built in 1912 and located at Regeringsgatan 9 (Figure 94), is an almost perfect restatement of the principles of the Chicago School. With its beautifully proportioned bays and large glass area, it appears especially close to the structural expressionism of Louis Sullivan. Where Nilsson encountered Sullivan (or perhaps Holabird & Roche) is not known, but according to Linn, it is probable that he knew them through magazine publication. In any event, he here created one of the most distinguished business buildings in the city of Stockholm — and one that very clearly reveals an American ancestry.

In Denmark Anton Rosen (1859–1928) played a role analogous to that of Boberg in Sweden. While Rosen was certainly one of the leading Danish architects of his time, he was overshadowed by the figure of Martin Nyrop, who built the Copenhagen Town Hall (Figure 95). This structure, which was by far the most important building project of its time in Denmark, ensured the preeminence of Nyrop and drew attention away from Rosen, who was much the more interesting architect. The two men were, in fact, temperamental opposites in almost every way. With the exception of a single trip to Italy, Nyrop never traveled, never read foreign magazines, and was totally absorbed in a romantic preoccupation with the Danish past. Indeed, he went so far in this direction that he adorned the town hall with stone walruses and polar bears that were symbolic of his country's Arctic possessions. Not surprisingly, Nyrop hated what he understood to be the modern European architecture of his day and actually went so far as to forbid his students at the Royal Academy of Fine Arts to read periodicals that featured it. He was especially bitter against Finnish magazines. Within his own office he seems to have adopted a kindly and congenial manner that concealed an extremely arbitrary character.[7]

Rosen (Figure 96) was altogether different in his outlook on

Figure 94
George Nilsson, business
building at Regeringsgatan
9, Stockholm, 1912

Figure 95
Martin Nyrop, Copenhagen
Town Hall, 1892–1905

Figure 96
Anton Rosen

Figure 97
Anton Rosen, workers' clubhouse, Silkeborg, Denmark,
1895

architecture and on life. In his student days and as a young man he traveled widely in Scandinavia and Western Europe, visiting France, Spain, Italy, Sweden, Norway, and Finland. Like Boberg, he was a close follower of international developments and evidently thought that salvation for Danish architecture lay in turning outward to the rest of the world. In this respect it may be noted that Denmark, like Sweden, underwent a cultural crisis in the nineteenth century that probably affected Rosen's thinking. While agriculture in Denmark was never in such a depressed condition as that in Sweden, the country had to cede the provinces of Schleswig and Holstein to Germany in the 1864 war with Prussia, and this loss was a profound shock. To compensate for the lost territories the nation launched an energetic program to reclaim arable land in Jutland and undertook a kind of cultural self-examination in various other ways. The Grundtvig movement within the Lutheran Church and the intensive development of the Danish folk high school were part of this effort. A good many Danes, among them Rosen, obviously thought that Denmark had been too long isolated from Europe and that it was time to become part of the Continent again. In consequence the atmosphere of Rosen's office was entirely different from that of Nyrop's. It attracted the best minds among the younger generation of Danish architects. Kay Fisker, Aage Rafn, and Svend Møller all worked there, as did Lars Sonck, the powerful Finnish contemporary of Eliel Saarinen. These young men all went on to distinguished careers, whereas none of Nyrop's students achieved much eminence.

Rosen's first years in practice were passed in Silkeborg, a small town in Jutland, where he married the daughter of the local hotel proprietor. One of his most interesting buildings, a worker's clubhouse, dates from 1895 and was distinctively Sullivanian in feeling (Figure 97). Unfortunately, it is known only through old photographs, as it was destroyed by the Germans during the Second World War. Also extremely provocative is the furniture done by Rosen for a hospital in

Silkeborg (Figure 98). The large wardrobe, which is a kind of scaled-down version of the Wainwright Building, might well have come from the Sullivan office or perhaps from that of Purcell and Elmslie. Obviously it was Sullivan rather than Richardson who meant something to Rosen, and we may well ask how he acquired his knowledge of the Chicago master.

Here there is an obvious connecting link in the shape of Alfred Ravad, a Danish architect who came to Chicago in 1890 and remained in that city until 1914. Ravad, who later went on to a noteworthy career in town planning in his native country, wrote a lengthy and well-illustrated essay on "American Architecture and Louis Sullivan" in *Tidskrift vor kunstindustrie* in 1898 (vol. 4, pp. 189–200). Ravad had been largely disappointed by the 1893 World's Fair. Sullivan's Transportation Building, however, was a revelation. The strong architectonic lines of its surfaces and the lavish decorations of the famous "Golden Door" were something entirely new and a portent of the future. The article also shows the Auditorium Hotel, Charnley House, and the Guaranty Building in Buffalo. Ravad evidently knew Sullivan well and succumbed to the somewhat hypnotic quality of his personality. He writes lyrically of the American's conception of architecture as poetry and of nature as a source of artistic inspiration. Some years later, when Sullivan's career had taken a downward turn, he wrote an enthusiastic notice of the publication of Sullivan's *Kindergarten Chats* for the Danish magazine *Arkitektur.*

It should be noted here that the editors of Scandinavian architectural magazines made a reasonable effort to keep their readers informed of developments on the American architectural scene but that in general they tended to limit themselves to coverage of technological innovations and of the official work. *Arkitektur,* for example, was much interested in American innovations in fireproof construction and published the neoclassical buildings at the St. Louis World's

Figure 98
Anton Rosen, furniture done
for hospital in Silkeborg,
Denmark, 1902

Figure 99
Anton Rosen, Palace Hotel,
Copenhagen, 1909

Figure 100
Anton Rosen, Savoy Hotel,
Copenhagen, 1912

VESTERBROGADE 34.   ARCHITEKT ANTON ROSEN.

Figure 101
Anton Rosen, Savoy Hotel,
Copenhagen, sketch of
facade and structural detail,
1912

Fair of 1904 in some detail. In somewhat similar fashion the
Swedish *Arkitektur* reported Walter Burley Griffin's victory
in the Canberra competition of 1912 very fully and also
carried an article by Ivar Kreuger, who was to become one
of the great swindlers of modern times, on American improvements in reinforced concrete construction. Kreuger
was much impressed by the work of Albert Kahn in this field.
Boberg and Ravad therefore performed a real service in
bringing the work of Richardson and Sullivan to their
countrymen. Except for a series of lectures by Professor
Wilhelm Wanscher at the Royal Academy in Copenhagen in
1910, there does not appear to have been any notice of the
work of Wright in Scandinavia.[8]

   After Rosen's move to Copenhagen he enjoyed a substantial practice though he was always overshadowed by Nyrop
and his school. His best-known work was the Palace Hotel
(Figure 99), whose individual and imaginative form, rich
brick ornamentation, and highly original interior (now
unhappily rebuilt) put it on a par with the best buildings in
Europe of its time. Showing a strong German influence from
Riemerschmid and Bruno Paul, the hotel was nonetheless
extremely Danish, especially in the fine finishing of its interior. Rosen designed all of its details down to the ashtrays
and the uniforms of the personnel. More interesting from the
American point of view, however, is the Savoy Hotel (Figures
100 and 101). For this structure, built in 1906, Rosen used
an extremely elegant skeleton construction and large areas
of glass. The frame was sheathed in bronze, and the ornamentation has the strongly appliqué feeling that is so
characteristic of Sullivan. In fact, the building may not un-
reasonably be compared with some of the best work of the
Chicago School. While it has not been well maintained, it
still adds considerable distinction to the street on which it
is located (Vesterbrogade), and it will certainly seem a
familiar type to any architecturally minded visitor from
America.

Rosen's other buildings in Copenhagen are a curiously mixed lot. Some, like the powerful, concrete-framed Metropole Theatre, are very much in the Jugend tradition; others are quite nondescript. One is led to the conclusion that Rosen's major difficulty may well have been that he was too open to ideas from abroad. Rejecting Nyrop's romantic preoccupation with the national past, he was unable to find firm ground on which to base himself. Hence his work is extremely uneven in quality. His last projects, such as his entry in the *Chicago Tribune* Competition of 1922, show an attempt to come to grips with the emerging international style of the 1920s. He also devoted a certain amount of time to the affairs of the Royal Academy of Fine Arts, of which he was president for a few years, but here, too, his position was undercut by the members of the Danish architectural establishment. Although he wanted to teach and was evidently a gifted teacher, he never had the opportunity to present his ideas in the classroom. Instead his influence was felt in the work of a few strong disciples such as Fisker and Møller, who always professed the highest regard for him. He died, a rather embittered man, in 1928.

We conclude, then, that Swedish and Danish architects were aware of, and influenced by, Richardson and Sullivan in the nineties and the first decade of this century. Richardson seems to have been of particular importance. His style is the basis of a surprising number of later developments. It also appears that our concept of an easy transition from historicism to a modern vernacular in the Scandinavian countries is misleading. In Sweden and Denmark, at any rate, there was a real struggle between an avant-garde, which wanted to bring architecture into line with the requirements of the twentieth century, and an establishment, which wanted to preserve the traditions of the national past. The avant-garde identified with progressive American architectural design, but the establishment won the battle. Its monuments are the Copenhagen and Stockholm town halls. Whoever wants to understand the history of modern architecture in Scandinavia must, however, begin by looking beyond these buildings.

It is therefore not surprising to find some startling similarities between the careers of Boberg, Rosen, and Sullivan. All three men pitted themselves against the establishments in their respective countries, and all were defeated, though the shock of defeat was not equally severe. With Sullivan the enemy was the academic classicism of the East as represented by McKim, Mead, and White; with Boberg and Rosen it was the national romanticism of Östberg and Nyrop. The struggles, however, had a remarkable similarity. In Boberg's case defeat was essentially seduction by an aristocracy and was cushioned by a very real interest in architectural history. Rosen was simply denied the opportunity, which should have been his, to expound his views at the Royal Academy. With Sullivan, defeat was especially bitter because of personal factors (an unhappy marriage and the problem of alcoholism) and the fact that for a few years in the nineties the cause actually appeared to be triumphant. He himself wrote in *The Autobiography of an Idea* that "the flag was flying in the breeze." During the First World War it became perfectly clear that the cause was lost for at least a generation.

It is significant that all three men have been honored by their respective countries in recent years. A Swedish book on Boberg appeared in 1958, and further publication is in prospect. Rosen's centennial was observed by the Danes with an exhibition, and a large variety of tributes to him also appeared in newspapers and magazines. In his excellent *History of Danish Architecture,* Tobias Faber, the new Rector of the Royal Academy, gives ample space to Rosen and bewails the fact that he was a lonely figure in Danish architecture. Sullivan's centennial in 1956 was celebrated with a large exhibition of his work at the Chicago Art Institute and a spate of articles in newspapers and magazines. Since that date the Sullivan bibliography has been increasing. No less than five books on various aspects of his career have been published, and there is no end in sight to what is, in the circumstances, a veritable flood of literature. Louis Sullivan is, in fact, well on his way to becoming a kind of folk hero for American architects.

The Scandinavian story, then, reinforces the conclusion that architectural innovators had a difficult time of it all over the Western world in the years around 1900. It required a special type of personality, like Nilsson in Sweden, Perret in France, or Frank Lloyd Wright in the United States, to survive the highly organized opposition of the establishment.

Notes

1. G. E. Kidder Smith, *Sweden Builds* (New York, 1957), p. 58.

2. Johnny Roosval, *Swedish Art* (Princeton, 1932), p. 73.

3. Marianne Moberg, "Djursholm, Sveriges forsta villasted De forsta villorna och deres ursprung," master's thesis, Stockholm University, 1965. Unhappily no English summary is available.

4. Hans Edestrand and Erik Lundberg, *Isak Gustaf Clason* (Stockholm, 1968), p. 167. The quotation is from the English summary. There is some reason to believe that Clason's most Richardsonian building was the Central Telephone Exchange in Warsaw of 1908. This building was published in *Ochrona zabytkow,* February 1969, p. 93, but I have not been able to obtain a good photograph for study.

5. Ulla Ehrensvard, *De svenske i Chicago 1893* (Stockholm, 1966). An English summary is provided.

6. Bjorn Linn, "Den stilsamme revolutionären," *Arkitektur: The Swedish Review of Architecture* 7 (July 1964): 157–169. English summary, p. vi.

7. My interpretation of Nyrop and Rosen owes much to conversations with the late Kay Fisker in October 1962 and August 1965. Fisker knew both men well.

8. Two photographs of Wright's Larkin Building of 1905 appear without comment in Gregor Paulsson, *Den ny arkitektur* (Copenhagen, 1920). I have been unable to find any other notice of Wright in any Danish or Swedish publication of the period.

6

Finnish Architecture:
The Richardsonian
Phase

Among architectural historians Eliel Saarinen's respect for Louis Sullivan is well known. When Saarinen first saw a picture of Sullivan's Transportation Building for the Chicago World's Fair of 1893, he clipped it from the newspaper in which it appeared and pinned it up above his drafting board. For him it was superb example of the freedom that he was seeking in his own work. Not so well known but even more important is the fact that Saarinen had an equally high regard for the architecture of H. H. Richardson. In 1947 the Danish architect Kay Fisker asked Saarinen about the importance of Sullivan and was somewhat startled to hear the elder man respond that for his generation Richardson was even more significant (Figure 102). He was, indeed, a key figure for a whole generation of Finnish architects.[1]

How did the influence of Richardson come to affect events in this distant corner of Europe? The answer to this query necessarily involves a consideration of certain aspects of Finnish cultural history. The keynote of that history in the late nineteenth century is an intense search for national identity. Until 1809 Finland had been a Swedish province; after that date it was a grand duchy within the Russian empire, enjoying substantial autonomy in the conduct of its internal affairs until the decade of the 1890s, when the increasingly repressive Romanov dynasty began a campaign of Russification. The petitions of the Finnish Diet were disregarded in St. Petersburg. Finnish economic privileges within the empire were curtailed, and, most distasteful of all, Finnish youths now had to serve in the Russian army. All of these measures ran counter to the development of Finnish nationalism that can conveniently be dated from 1835, the year in which Elias Lonnrot published the first edition of the national folk epic, the *Kalevala*. As I have observed elsewhere, this was an event of profound significance.[2] Lonnrot's publication gave status to the Finnish language, which had hitherto been the tongue of peasants and fishermen. Within little more than a generation, Finnish attained equal

Figure 102
Mr. and Mrs. Eliel Saarinen
on board the Kungsholm,
1935

status with Swedish as a legal and literary language, and writers, painters, musicians, and architects became preoccupied with the *Kalevala.* The magnificent tone poems of Jean Sibelius on themes from the epic are well known, and the painter Aksel Gallén-Kallela (1865–1931) devoted years of his life to illustrating it. Gallén-Kallela, in fact, fixed the image of the heroes and heroines of the *Kalevala* so firmly in the national mind that Finns today cannot imagine them apart from his paintings. The elder Saarinen also knew the poem well and as a young man even traveled through Karelia (Finland's easternmost province) seeking out the rune singers. All these artists felt a compulsion to be Finnish, which was the more intense because it was relatively new. An acute Finnish statesman once remarked, "We cannot any longer be Swedes; we do not wish to be Russians; therefore, we must be Finns." This was all very well, but what was a Finn? Superficially the answer might be that he was someone who lived in Finland, spoke Finnish, and knew the *Kalevala,* but this would scarcely satisfy a searching inquiry. It was left for the generation of Lars Sonck and Eliel Saarinen to define the Finnish character in terms of architecture.

At this point it is well to observe that Finland had in the late nineteenth century a fair-sized body of architecture that belonged to two important European building traditions. The first was the Gothic, exemplified by the brick-built cathedral of Turku and echoed in a number of smaller country churches such as the one at Eckerö in the Åland Islands, a thirteenth-century creation (Figure 103). As can easily be seen these structures generally incorporate a good deal of extremely roughhewn masonry. The other style that was well represented in the country was the neoclassicism of the early nineteenth century, whose chief exponent was Carl Ludwig Engel. A schoolmate of Friedrich Gilly in Berlin and a contemporary of the great Schinkel, Engel was one of the most gifted architects of his generation. While Engel built all over Finland, he is best known for his design of the Cathe-

Figure 103
Thirteenth-century church
at Eckerö, Åland Islands

Figure 104
Carl Ludwig Engel, Holy
Trinity Church, Helsinski,
1827

Figure 105
Carl Ludwig Engel, Senate
Building, Helsinki, 1822

Figure 106
Carl Ludwig Engel, Senate
Building, corner pavilion,
Helsinki, 1822

dral Square in Helsinki. The structures on three sides of this splendid area are his, and he made it into one of the finest public open spaces in Europe. On close examination Engel turns out to be a master of wall architecture in the grand tradition of the Renaissance. His beautifully proportioned, marvelously articulated surfaces will easily bear comparison with the best Italian work of the sixteenth and seventeenth centuries. Spatially he was also a master, as the superb interior volumes of the National Cathedral demonstrate very clearly, and when confronted with a small problem containing a difficult economic factor, he was equally effective. Here the wooden church of the Holy Trinity in Helsinki is a good example (Figure 104). The one thing that Engel never did, however, was to employ a rough texture in the walls of his public buildings. A study of the walls of his Senate Building will reveal that it is composed of smooth, well-cut, regular units of ashlar (Figures 105 and 106). It therefore differs radically from the walls that Sonck, Saarinen, and their contemporaries were to develop in the period 1895–1910. We must, then, consider the Finnish architecture of these years as one aspect of the search for national identity and as a reaction against Engel, who, highly respected as he was, had, after all, worked for a Russian governor-general. Here is the explanation of the Finnish fondness for Richardson.

While no Finnish writer has, so far as I know, commented on the matter, granite is for the Finns both an important building material and a significant national symbol. Finland was one of the most thoroughly glaciated areas in Europe, and when the glaciers receded about ten thousand years ago, they left granite behind them in abundance. With pine, birch, and water, it is one of the principal elements of the Finnish landscape. The traveler in the country will soon become accustomed to huge, lichen-covered granite boulders in the forests and to stone walls on farms, laid up much as in New England. In the Helsinki townscape granite is also a pervasive element. Landscape designers often uncover it and use it with great effectiveness in the city parks. The Sibelius Park in Helsinki is especially noteworthy in this respect. Sometimes architects also take advantage of it as a landscape backdrop for their buildings. A series of houses with courtyards by Jaako Laappotti in the suburb of Haga is a good example (Figure 107). Here the earth has been scraped off and the granite has been made into an attractive playground for the local children. The area gets hard use, since it is a natural setting for games such as King of the Hill. The children in this neighborhood literally grow up on granite.

Additional evidence of the importance of the granite symbol in Finnish life is easy to find. The famous Finnish *sisu* is commonly defined as "that quality which enables a man to walk through gray granite." *Sisu,* it may be observed, is one of the four Finnish words that have achieved some degree of international acceptance. The others are *sauna, puuku* (the long Finnish woodsman's knife), and *rapakivi.* This last refers to a special kind of granite, notable for its unusual crystalline structure, which was first found around Viipuri and the shores of the Gulf of Finland. Since its identification and description in that area, it has been discovered in a good many other parts of the world, and the Finnish term has been taken over by geologists. Of these four words, then, two refer to granite.

If we ask, "What are the qualities of granite as a symbol?" there are several possible answers. In the first place, it suggests hardness, obduracy, and extreme stubbornness. It is not a material that is easily worked by the sculptor; in the entire history of European sculpture there are only a few periods in which much work has been done in granite. For the mason and architect it also presents formidable problems, although these are somewhat diminished by the use of modern equipment. In any event, it is certainly a material with great toughness and resistance to shock. It may be noted that these are precisely the qualities needed by a small na-

Figure 107
Landscape playground area
at rear of Orapihlajatie
housing by Jaako Laappotti,
Helsinki, 1963

tion situated between two expanding, aggressive, powers. For several hundred years this was Finland's situation vis-à-vis Sweden and Russia. In the early eighteenth century the population was decimated in the wars between these two countries; Finnish historians have sometimes grimly characterized their nation's role at this time as "Sweden's bloody shield." It is not pleasant to be a buffer state. Psychologically speaking, we can say that granite is an excellent symbol for those qualities of mind and heart that the Finns have needed in order to preserve and develop their national identity.

We may also observe that granite lends itself to a kind of rough textural treatment that is characteristic of many aspects of Finnish life. (Note the surface of the *ryijy* rug.) A nation reveals itself by the qualities that it prizes in its public men. Traditionally the French demand intellectual brilliance in their political leaders; the English want force of character and skill in debate. What qualities do the Finns prefer? The answer to this question was suggested to me by a Finnish friend one day in casual conversation. He said, "We like our public men to be a bit rough." By this phrase he conveyed the idea that a certain hardness of demeanor was desirable. Affability, intellectual achievement, and quickness in response were not as valuable as ruggedness and stubbornness. If one observes Finnish political life, he will notice that the men who achieve high office display these qualities to a surprising degree. Marshal Mannerheim and President Juho Paasikivi were certainly notable in these respects, nor is Mr. Kekkonen lacking here. It may perhaps be a bit unusual to make so psychological an interpretation of a building material, but in this case it is difficult to ignore the implications of its use.

The cultural situation that I have just outlined caused Finnish architects to become conscious of European and American developments to a remarkable degree. Even more than their colleagues in Denmark and Sweden, they followed

the most advanced designs of the 1890s and early 1900s
in European architectural periodicals. A good example of
their attitude is to be found in an address given by Bertil
Jung on March 2, 1901, at a meeting of the Finnish Technical
Society. Jung showed complete familiarity with the work of
William Morris in England, of van de Velde in Belgium and
Germany, and most important of all, of Otto Wagner in Vienna. While Jung seems to have felt that Finland was at the
moment somewhat behind the other nations of Europe, he
anticipated a bright future. Two other articles in the Finnish
architectural press during the early years of the century
dealt with "The City of New York" and "American Building";
their authors, Ludvig Mallander and Thor Lagerros, be-
moaned the fact that the Americans had not yet freed themselves from the tyranny of European architectural styles.
Unfortunately, neither man seems to have penetrated the
country as far inland as Chicago, but Mallander expresses
a great regard for Richardson.

   In the light of this climate of opinion, the exact source of
the Finnish knowledge of Richardson is unimportant. It may
have come through Sweden, where the Richardsonian work
of Boberg was extensively published in the nineties. Another
possible source is in the German and English publications
on Richardson. In any event, it is perfectly clear that the
American architect had a great impact in Finland in the
period 1890–1914. Perhaps the most striking change in
style is to be found in the work of Professor Gustaf Nyström,
one of the country's leading teachers of architecture. Nyström's National Archives Building in Helsinki of 1890 is a
good example of the refined classicism that derived from
Engel (Figure 108). In 1904, shortly before he died, Nystrom
did an art gallery for the city of Turku (Figure 109). There
could hardly be a greater contrast between two buildings.
One seems still to belong to the early nineteenth century
while the other is protomodern. The smooth surfaces of
regularly cut ashlar have been replaced by powerful boul-

Figure 108
Professor Gustaf Nyström,
National Archives Building,
Helsinki, 1890

Figure 109
Professor Gustaf Nyström,
Art Gallery, Turku, Finland,
1904

Figure 110
Karl Hård af Segerstadt,
Market Hall, Viipuri,
Finland, 1906

Figure 111
Karl Hård af Segerstadt,
Clubhouse for Foreign
Students, Helsinki, 1901

Figure 112
Lindahl and Thomé,
Clubhouse for Students of
Technical University,
Helsinki, 1903

ders whose rough textures force themselves upon the observer. The delicately scaled series of terraces by which the architect leads the viewer up to the entrance of the museum is especially fine.

The architect who was probably closest to Boberg in Sweden was Karl Hård af Segerstadt. The entry to his Market Hall for Viipuri of 1906 (Figure 110) might be mistaken for almost any public building in an American town where Richardsonian influence was strong. A detail of the polychrome stonework above the archway would resemble any one of several portions of Richardson's Trinity Church in Boston, and the fenestration is also decidedly Richardsonian. In Helsinki, Hård af Segerstadt did a student clubhouse (1901) (Figure 111) that is in the same vein. It is well to note that Richardson was, of course, not the only foreign influence on Finnish architects during these crucial years. Gontran Goulden, Director of the Building Centre, London, has alluded to ". . . the strange and interesting group of buildings dating from the early days of this century when the spirit of National Romanticism was fiercely burning. . . . Many of these buildings have a strong, rugged, almost fortresslike appearance, others are curiously Scottish baronial in handling and some, particularly by Saarinen, remind me of Glasgow and Charles Rennie Mackintosh."[3] It is quite natural that an Englishman would see this body of architecture in terms of Scottish precedent. Close visual examination, however, will indicate that Richardson was even more important than the Scottish baronial style. The surface here is in the same rough masonry seen in the Art Museum, and the window rhythms are again very Richardsonian. Another even more striking building of the same type is the clubhouse for the students of the Technical University of Finland by Lindahl and Thomé in 1909 (Figure 112). This remarkable structure, always known simply as "the Poly," preserves the Richardsonian surfaces and fenestration, which were by this date quite common, but substitutes for the older round arches a pointed arch with a curious stilted profile. These arches, which also occur in the work of Lars Sonck, seem to be a distinctively Finnish characteristic. The round towers are nicely integrated into the facade (as in Richardson's Stoughton house, Cambridge, 1885), and the structure possesses a number of fascinating interior details, such as the piers composed of rough-cut boulders (Figure 113).

Of all the Finnish architects of this generation the man who most creatively absorbed the message of Richardson was Lars Sonck, who is only now beginning to receive the attention that he merits. His two most significant works in this respect are undoubtedly the Telephone Building in Helsinki of 1905 (Figures 114 and 115), and the Lutheran Cathedral at Tampere (Figures 116 and 117). The Telephone Building presents a powerfully composed facade of that Finnish granite which, as Siegfried Giedion noted, was well suited to Sonck's personality. (He was known to his contemporaries as "the big man with a firm hand.") Always an architect of willful originality, Sonck truncated his arches in a distinctive manner and added a number of unique decorative touches. For the cathedral he used the familiar rough-hewn masonry and a remarkable western window that a few years ago attracted the attention of Professor Hitchcock.[4] Unhappily the excellent interior space of this building is marred by one of the characteristically dreadful murals of the period.

The firm of Gesellius, Lindgren, and Saarinen was equally interested in American work at the turn of the century. The earliest Richardsonian structure by the partners is probably the headquarters for the Pohjola Insurance Company in 1901 (Figures 118 and 119). The facade treatment, the stubby tower, and the fenestration all derive from Richardson. It is, of course, a building with a strong connection to the national epic. Pohjola and Kullervo are two of the leading characters in the *Kalevala,* and their grinning, gargoylelike features appear around the entrance. Also extremely Rich-

Figure 113
Lindahl and Thomé,
Clubhouse for Students of
Technical University, inter-
ior detail, Helsinki, 1903

Figure 114
Lars Sonck, Telephone
Building, Helsinki, 1905

Figure 115
Lars Sonck, Telephone
Building, detail of facade,
Helsinki, 1905

Figure 116
Lars Sonck, Lutheran
Cathedral, Tampere,
Finland, 1908

Figure 119
Gesellius, Lindgren, and
Saarinen, Pohjola Insurance
Company, doorway, Helsinki,
1901

Figure 120
Gesellius, Lindgren, and
Saarinen, Suur-Merijoki
near Viipuri, 1903

Figure 121
Architect's drawing,
Suur-Merijoki, 1903

Figure 125
Eliel Saarinen, Town Hall,
Lahti, Finland, 1912

Figure 123
Gesellius, Lindgren, and
Saarinen, second prize project for National Theater,
Helsinki, 1898

Figure 124
Eliel Saarinen, project
(second prize) in "Haus
eines Kunstfreundes" competition, Essen, Germany,
1904

Figure 126
Eliel Saarinen, Town Hall,
entrance, Lahti, Finland,
1912

Figure 127
Onni Tarjanne, National
Theater, Helsinki, 1902

ardsonian is the large country house that the partners built
for a client at Suur-Merijoki near Viipuri in 1903 (Figures
120 and 121). In this building the reference is specifically
to the architectural dispositions in Richardson's gate lodge
for the Ames family in North Easton, Massachusetts, of
1880–1881 (Figure 122). There the wall treatment, in boulders, is, however, even stronger than the squared rubble of
the Finnish building.[5]

About 1904 a decisive shift occurred in the style of Gesellius, Lindgren, and Saarinen. In general this shift involved a
movement away from American precedent and an increasing
interest in German and Austrian developments. As early as
1898 a competition project for a national theater in Helsinki
had been distinctly Wagnerian in character (Figure 123).
Now projects such as Saarinen's entry in the "Haus eines
Kunstfreundes" competition of 1904 show an orientation
toward the work of Olbrich in Darmstadt (Figure 124). The
crucial event was probably the firm's victory in the Helsinki
railroad station competition of 1904. After this triumph
Saarinen traveled extensively on the Continent, partly on
vacation and partly for professional reasons. His biographer
noted that in 1907 he visited Joseph Olbrich in Darmstadt
and Peter Behrens in Düsseldorf and that he was particularly
interested in Behrens's interiors and in his furniture design.[6]
These contacts obviously had an effect.

Hence the Saarinen office moved away from the neo-Rich-
ardsonian manner to an architecture more in keeping with
the latest Continental developments. A good example of
this new style is the town hall that Saarinen built for Lahti,
an industrial city about seventy-five miles north of Helsinki.
(Figures 125 and 126). In this large structure, which occupies
an entire city block, the roughhewn granite walling is replaced by smooth brickwork and a first floor of rather grainy
local ashlar. Only the plan, which is arranged around an
interior courtyard and has a curious resemblance to that
of the Allegheny County Courthouse, is in any way Richard-

sonian. The handling of the ornament around the doorway is somewhat reminiscent of Otto Wagner. The tower, which became a kind of ideogram with Saarinen, bestows monumentality on the edifice; those familiar with his buildings at Cranbrook will easily recognize it as the prototype of the tower on the boys' school there. A good many of the brick details will also be familiar.

Perhaps the largest single monument in the Richardsonian phase of Finnish architecture was the National Theatre in Helsinki done by Onni Tarjanne in 1902 (Figure 127). The round arches and the rough masonry seem rather hackneyed, and it is not surprising to find the Saarinen office turning away from the style in their designs of the next decade.

In sum, Richardson was for Finnish architects a fruitful source of inspiration. In Sullivan they found a spirit of freedom and release from tradition, but in Richardson they found a method of handling masonry and a kind of design that harmonized nicely with their own objectives. When evaluating the impact of these two American architects, however, it is well to remember the wise words of the late Carl Becker:

It has long been a favorite pastime of those who interest themselves in the history of culture to note the transfer of ideas (as if it were no more than a matter of borrowed coins) from one writer, for example, that Mr. Jones must have got a certain idea from Mr. Smith, because it can be shown that he reads or might have read, Mr. Smith's book; all the while forgetting that if Mr. Jones hadn't already had the idea or something like it, simmering in his own mind, he wouldn't have cared to read Mr. Smith's book, or having read it, would very likely have thrown it aside, or written a review to show what a bad and mistaken book it was. [7]

The Finns took to Sullivan and Richardson because they were ready for them.

Notes

1. Albert Christ-Janer, *Eliel Saarinen* (Chicago, 1948), p. 10; conversation with Kay Fisker, August 1965. Fisker recalled that Saarinen was a handsome old man with the manners of a mandarin.

2. Leonard K. Eaton, "Finnish Architecture: Traditions and Development," *Progressive Architecture* 15 (April 1964): 154–161.

3. Gontran Goulden, "To Helsinki with an Architect's Love," *Look at Finland,* spring quarter 1965, p. 4.

4. Henry-Russell Hitchcock, "Aalto versus Aalto: The Other Finland," *Perspecta,* nos. 9–10 (1965), pp. 132–166.

5. Marika Hausen, "Gesellius-Lindgren-Saarinen vid sekelskiftet," *Arkkitehti-Arkitekten* 9 (1967): 6–12. The author supplies an English translation, and she emphasizes the work of the other partners equally with that of Saarinen.

6. Christ-Janer, *Saarinen,* p. 18.

7. Carl Becker, *The Heavenly City of the Eighteenth Century Philosophers* (New Haven, 1932), p. 72.

7

Louis Sullivan and
Hendrik Berlage

In July 1906, William Gray Purcell, a young American architect who had worked in the office of Louis Sullivan and long admired what Sullivan stood for, called at the architectural office of Dr. Hendrik P. Berlage in Amsterdam. At that time, the famous Amsterdam stock exchange had just been finished, and it is not surprising that Purcell should have wanted to meet its designer, who was clearly recognized as one of the most influential and controversial architects in Europe. Purcell found him to be a little man, formally dressed in a Prince Albert coat with a square-cut shirt, stiff collar, and black tie. He had a serious face, penetrating eyes, a pointed gray beard, and altogether looked much like a conventional European college professor (Figure 128). Notwithstanding this formality of bearing, he was lively and imaginative, full of enthusiasm, and spent the better part of two days showing Purcell and George Feick, his traveling companion, his works in Amsterdam and The Hague. He spoke English well enough to carry on a comfortable conversation.

Berlage's first questions to his young American visitors were, somewhat surprisingly, not about architecture but about Theodore Roosevelt. The inimitable "Teddy," the greatest American international figure of his day, had captured the imaginations of people everywhere; Europeans naturally wanted to know if he was really as fabulous as the newspaper stories led them to believe. In addition, Berlage, who was a convinced socialist all his life, was interested in Roosevelt's efforts to "bust the trusts." Next, the conversation turned to the new American architecture of Louis Sullivan and Frank Lloyd Wright. Purcell recalled that Berlage was well informed about both these men, had studied their work thoroughly, and was conversant with their architectural philosophy. As they went about from place to place, a considerable part of the discussion revolved about the work of the two great Midwestern pioneers. Like Eliel Saarinen, who tacked a picture of it above his drafting board, Berlage had been much impressed by Sullivan's Transportation Building

Figure 128
Hendrik P. Berlage, ca.
1906

at the Chicago World's Fair of 1893. He was also familiar with the excellent publication of Wright's work in *Architectural Review* (Boston) in 1900, and had seen some of Sullivan's writings. At the time of this meeting in 1906 he had been interested in American architecture for many years. He told Purcell that he had great hopes of coming to America and seeing the work of these two men for himself but that he had no idea when he would be able to make such an expensive journey. Purcell replied that insofar as his business permitted he would be glad to go about with Dr. Berlage, introduce him to the men he wanted to see, and show him their work. This promise had important consequences a few years later.[1]

In the spring of 1911, Berlage's affairs were in such condition that he could contemplate an extensive trip, and he proceeded to get in touch with William B. Feakins, the manager of a New York lecture bureau that represented such celebrities as Estelle Sylvia Pankhurst, the prominent English suffragette; the actress Beatrice Forbes-Robertson; and Fola LaFollette. He proposed to give a series of lectures in the United States which would "treat of architecture; more especially in connection with the other arts and the entire social evolution." After some correspondence with Purcell, Feakins undertook the management of Berlage's American tour, and the Dutch architect set sail from Rotterdam on October 28, 1911, to make his long-desired journey. He arrived in New York about ten days later; the first evidence of his presence in the United States is a revealing interview in *The New York Herald* of November 12, 1911. Following the arresting caption, "Criticized Dutch Architect Criticizes New York Architecture," the writer states that Dr. H. P. Berlage, designer of the much-criticized Bourse in Amsterdam, was in the United States to study the architecture of New York, Washington, Boston, Philadelphia, Chicago, Pittsburgh, and as many other cities as he had time to visit. The article contained some perceptive strictures on the New York architecture of that day. Berlage found the Public Library (Figure 129) "spacious and dignified but beautiful only as a copy"; he had hoped, he said, to see "an architecture less traditional in detail, more symbolic of America." The *New York Herald* building (Figure 130), he observed, was a copy of the Verona Town Hall, which did not really make much sense as the headquarters of a great modern newspaper. The rest of the article was in the same vein and was in fact so vigorous that it provoked a counterblast from four advocates of Beaux-Arts eclecticism in the next Sunday's *Herald:* Thomas Hastings of Carrère & Hastings, Benjamin W. Morris of LaFarge & Morris, and J. O. Post and W. S. Post of George Post & Sons. Typical of their remarks was the irate comment of Hastings: "No one, I believe, could accuse the library of being a direct copy from any building which has ever existed. If I understand his point of view, however, he believes that we should have a new style of our own. This in my opinion, is unphilosophical." Berlage's American journey had had a lively beginning.

Berlage lectured on "Art and the Community" at the League for Political Education on November 16 and then, in company with Purcell, who had come East on business, set out for Chicago. On arrival in that city the two men called on Louis Sullivan. When Sullivan learned that Berlage was going to Owatonna, Minnesota, to see the famous bank there and would return to Chicago in about a week, he invited him to call later when there would be more time available for discussion of their mutual interests. Sullivan, of course, knew about the Amsterdam Bourse and viewed it as a landmark of the new architecture. Purcell and Berlage spent the next two or three days sight-seeing in Chicago and Oak Park, taking in, among other buildings, Richardson's wholesale store for Marshall Field; the Auditorium Hotel; and the Garrick Theatre, Gage, and Carson, Pirie, Scott buildings. Berlage was particularly interested in the last named, and Purcell recalled:

It was plain that Dr. Berlage was a scholar and that no aspect

Figure 129
Carrère & Hastings, New
York Public Library,
1902–1909

Figure 130
McKim, Mead & White, New
York Herald Building,
1893–1894

or relation of what he was examining was allowed to pass un-
noticed. His questions were very penetrating and concerned
every aspect of the building—its plan, engineering, economic
relations, relation to the community, what people thought
about it, how the designs were produced, what was the background of the people who worked on it, the relation of Sullivan to his engineer—nothing escaped the man's examination, all done with scholarly seriousness and yet with a light
touch and pleasant conversation with occasionally some little humor creeping into the exchanges. A most agreeable
companion in every way.

The two men also called on Walter Burley Griffin, who was
just starting his competition design for the new Australian
city of Canberra; Berlage later wrote most approvingly of this
plan in the book that he published on his return to Holland.
The better part of a day was spent in Oak Park, where Frank
Lloyd Wright's studio was the major point of interest together
with his houses in the surrounding suburbs and the famous
Unity Temple. Wright himself was not available to greet his
distinguished visitor, and it was probably Isabel Roberts
who showed them through the Oak Park studio.
  From Chicago, the pair went north to Owatonna, inspected
Sullivan's bank there, and proceeded to Minneapolis, where
Berlage stayed in the Purcell home. There he visited the offices of Purcell and his partner, George Elmslie, who were
carrying on the Sullivan tradition in the Northwest; saw some
of their buildings; and lectured before an audience of about
two hundred people at the Handicraft Guild Hall. It is a sad
commentary on the state of American architecture at the
time that despite special invitations and the sponsorship of
the Minneapolis Society of Architects, only a few architects
other than members of the firm of Purcell and Elmslie were
in the house. The speech was, it should be added, well reported in the local press and was later published in *The
Western Architect.*
  At the conclusion of his stay in Minneapolis, Berlage returned to Chicago to deliver another lecture and to spend a
memorable evening with Sullivan listening to him read his

poetry until a late hour. Berlage, for whom writing was always a chore, greatly admired Sullivan's literary facility and completely understood his conception of the poetic qualities inherent in fine architecture. From Chicago, Berlage made his way eastward by way of Cleveland and Buffalo, stopping, in the latter city to see Wright's Larkin Building, which made a vast impression on him. He also visited Washington, D.C., to see the Capitol, which he found dull, matter-of-fact, and cold. He finished his American journey in New England, where he met members of the architectural faculties at Harvard and Yale and lectured in New Haven and Boston. An account of the Boston lecture in one of that city's leading papers, *The Boston Evening Transcript,* indicates that it must have been quite successful; the reporter wrote admiringly of the "magnificent central hall" of the Amsterdam Bourse.[2] After one more lecture for the Municipal Art Society of New York, before a large audience, on December 11, Berlage sailed for Holland, feeling that he had had an excellent trip. Feakins, who had managed his tour, attended the last lecture and heard numerous appreciative comments.

In retrospect, it appears that Dr. Berlage made an exceptionally thorough survey of the American architectural scene in a brief period of time. He met all the leading Chicago architects except Wright, who was then unavailable, and visited most of their important buildings. His only omission (and this was probably due to the pressure of time) was a visit to the Pacific Coast to make the acquaintance of Maybeck and the brothers Greene. His trip was well reported in the popular press, and the architectural journals gave it considerable publicity. His three lectures appeared in *The Western Architect* at about the same time they were published in a Dutch edition at Rotterdam, and his work was the subject of two articles in *The Craftsman* magazine. He met numerous nonarchitectural dignitaries, including President Taft and several of the leading faculty members of Harvard and Yale, and fulfilled a long-cherished ambition by speaking at length with ex-President Theodore Roosevelt at *The Outlook* offices in New York. All in all, the journey must be accounted a success.

Far more important than the effect of Berlage on America, however, was the impression of American architecture which he carried back to Europe with him. Soon after his return to the Netherlands, he began to deliver lectures on American architecture and held at his home a series of classes on the subject for the younger generation of Dutch architects. In conversation with this writer, the late J. J. P. Oud clearly remembered the enthusiasm with which Berlage spoke of Sullivan's Owatonna bank, of the Larkin Building, and of the various country houses of Wright. Coming from an acknowledged leader of the Modern Movement, this endorsement had a tremendous effect. Oud himself designed one or two projects of a strongly Wrightian character.

Even more important than Berlage's lectures were his published accounts of his journey. For European architecture at large, the more important of these was undoubtedly a pair of articles that appeared in *Schweizerische Bauzeitung* in 1912. With the Wasmuth publications of 1910, they were key elements in bringing Wright to the notice of advanced European architects. These articles must have come as a considerable shock to its readers. Beginning with the observation that most people thought of American architecture solely in terms of the skyscraper, Berlage stated that he had nevertheless found an American architecture entirely apart from this type of structure. He proposed to deal with the modern tradition in America as it appeared in the work of Richardson, Sullivan, and Wright. On Richardson, whom he resembled in many ways, Berlage was curiously hard.[3] Because of his use of Romanesque details, Richardson, he said, "very soon ceased to be regarded as a modern architect." For Sullivan, on the other hand, he had great sympathy. He dealt perceptively with Sullivan's treatment of the skyscraper and the department store, making, as one might expect, certain reservations about the famous Sullivan ornament. Sullivan's masterpiece was, in Berlage's mind, the bank at Owatonna, which, he observed, "cannot, as far as I am aware, be matched by anything similar on the European continent." For Wright, he reserved his encomiums, hailing him as "an architect of an especially high standing." While writing at length about Wright's series of distinguished country houses around Chicago, he was most enthusiastic about the Unity Temple and the Larkin Building in Buffalo. He analyzed both these structures in considerable detail and wrote in conclusion,

I returned thus from America with the conviction that there is in that country a new architecture that is in the process of evolution and that that architecture is already showing many successes. We Europeans have, in any case, little cause to regard American architecture as inferior. On the contrary, for the work of the best of America's architects reveals an originality and a power of perception which promise great developments in the future.[4]

While the articles in the Swiss magazine were directed toward a European audience, Berlage's *Amerikanische Reiseerinnerungen,* published at Rotterdam in 1913, probably had more meaning for his fellow countrymen. This volume is a much more extensive report of his journey and contains a number of shrewd observations on the American scene at large. Here Berlage devotes a good deal of attention to the problems of town planning in the United States and finds, incidentally, that in America, at any rate, the much-abused gridiron plan has a certain amount to be said for it. He has nothing but admiration for the boldness with which Americans tackle their gigantic problems and particularly cites the Chicago lakefront extension scheme as an example of courage and determination. As might be expected, Berlage extends his analysis of the works of Sullivan and Wright and even quotes at length from the writings of both men. Because he has arrived at similar opinions, he is especially taken with their views on the art of the classical, Gothic, and Renaissance periods. Most of all, however, he is moved by Wright's opposition to the views of Ruskin and

Morris on industrialism and by Wright's approach to the problems of a machine technology. As in the shorter German publication, he concludes that the future of American architecture is bright indeed.

The effect of Berlage's activity in behalf of the new American developments can be seen in a series of buildings scattered across the Netherlands. For the architecturally minded traveler, the evidence is everywhere. The offices of the local newspaper at Hilversum appear almost like one of Purcell and Elmslie's small-town banks picked up and set down three thousand miles away from its actual location (Figure 131). A comparison with the bank (1910) at Grand Meadow, Minnesota, reveals how close the resemblance is (Figure 132). A number of such buildings done during the decade of World War I demonstrate that the influence of Sullivan was particularly strong at this time. In Berlage's own work it is seen most clearly in the facade of Holland House (1914) in London (Figure 133). The architect wrote that since the municipality required a steel frame, he had solved the problem by covering it with glazed terra-cotta, "in accordance with the later construction of some of the American skyscrapers." The precedent for this design can be found in a number of Sullivan's multistoried office buildings. The Guaranty Building in Buffalo, also sheathed in terra cotta (1895) is a good example (Figure 134). Both the Dutch and American buildings display the same powerful treatment of the vertical elements. Berlage, of course, omits entirely the effervescent ornament that is so characteristic of Sullivan.

The most striking evidence of the impact that Sullivan had on Berlage occurs some years later in a Christian Science church designed at The Hague in 1925 (Figure 135). Berlage had always been somewhat radical in religious matters and on his visit to the United States had greatly admired Sullivan's startling design for St. Paul's Methodist Episcopal Church in Cedar Rapids, Iowa (Figures 136 and 137). Observing that the church authorities probably objected to the scheme in some degree, he stated approvingly that Sullivan had deviated completely from the conventional Protestant church plan. "Rightly starting from the recognition that a Protestant church has to be an ideal meeting-room," wrote Berlage, "he [Sullivan] made the auditorium in the form of a semi-circle, placing the tower in the center, that is, on the place of the pulpit. With this he therefore broke completely with the tradition of Protestant church-building, which has never quite been able to free itself from the form of the original Christian church, namely the Roman Catholic, whereas the tower by its special place receives a higher, ideal significance than that of bell tower alone." One cannot help wondering if Berlage was not here subconsciously reverting to the strong tradition of Dutch Protestantism in which the church is seen simply as an amphitheater for preaching.

In plan (Figure 138), Berlage's church is not a semicircle but a truncated triangle with the two readers required by the Christian Science service placed at the cutoff point. The floor slope is as steep as possible, to avoid the problem of steps and to ensure that each person in the audience will be able to see and hear the readers. A comparison with Sullivan's plan reveals that Berlage was not able to dispose of his masses in the same forceful manner as the American architect, probably because of the cramped nature of his site. Like Sullivan, Berlage placed the tower directly over the focal point of the service, in this case the desks of the two readers. It is as if Berlage had filed the Sullivan idea away for a number of years, and then, when the occasion arose, pulled it out of a cabinet. The interior has a cool, restful character very much in keeping with the quiet nature of the Christian Science ritual (Figure 139). The structure is thoroughly conventional, and a detail of the exterior shows that Berlage was still adhering to his beloved flat surfaces of brick and that the fenestration was somewhat petty in quality (Figure 140). Those who visit both buildings will probably prefer Sullivan's, even though the executed structure differs in several

Figure 131
J. Van Laren, newspaper
office at Hilversum, 1927

Figure 132
Purcell and Elmslie, First
State Bank, Grand Meadow,
Minnesota, 1910

Figure 135
Hendrik P. Berlage, First
Church of Christ, Scientist,
The Hague, 1925

Figure 136
Louis Sullivan, St. Paul's
Methodist Episcopal
Church, Cedar Rapids, Iowa,
1911

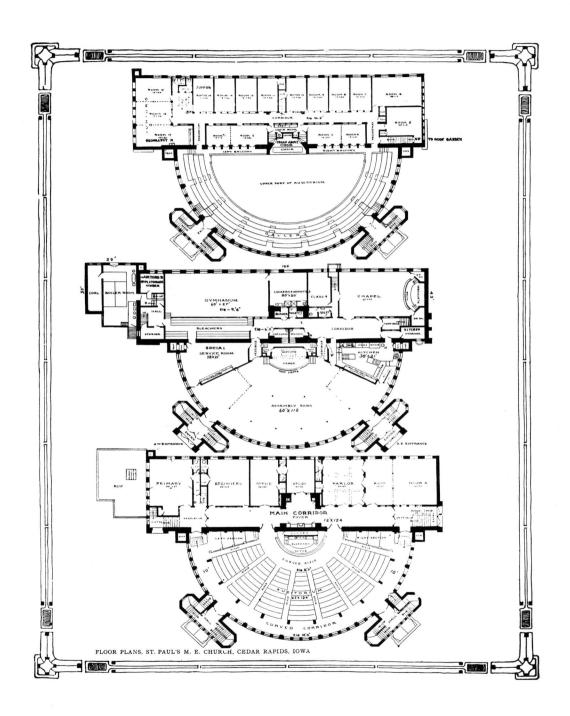

FLOOR PLANS, ST. PAUL'S M. E. CHURCH, CEDAR RAPIDS, IOWA

Figure 137
Louis Sullivan, St. Paul's
Methodist Episcopal
Church, Cedar Rapids, Iowa,
plan

Figure 138
Hendrik P. Berlage, First
Church of Christ, Scientist,
The Hague, plan

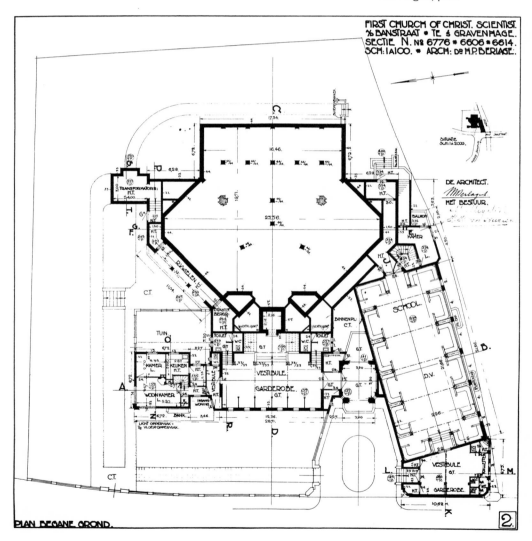

Figure 139
Hendrik P. Berlage, First
Church of Christ, Scientist,
The Hague, interior, 1925

Figure 140
Hendrik P. Berlage, First
Church of Christ, Scientist,
The Hague, rear elevation,
1925

Figure 141
Louis Sullivan, St. Paul's
Methodist Episcopal Church,
Cedar Rapids, Iowa, tower,
1911

Figure 142
Hendrik P. Berlage, shooting
lodge for the Kröller-Müller
family, Otterlo, 1915

important respects from the original design. The explanation for this variation is that the church building committee was frightened by the cost of Sullivan's design and hired W. C. Jones of Chicago to redraw the master's plans and bring them into line with the funds available to the congregation. Fortunately, George Elmslie was able to go over Jones's alterations and save most of Sullivan's church.

Finally, we should note the similarity between Sullivan's tower for the Cedar Rapids church and the tower that Berlage built for the shooting lodge he designed (1915) for the Kröller-Müller family at Otterlo (Figures 141 and 142). In both cases, the architects appear to have felt compelled to put "hats" on their towers rather than let them soar into the blue like Gothic steeples. The observation posts on Berlage's tower also bear a resemblance to the fenestration on Sullivan's which is more than coincidental.

The evidence, then, seems to indicate that in the crucial decade, 1910–1920, Dutch architects tended to think of the new American architecture as the product of a school rather than of a single man. Berlage, at any rate, was a good deal more attracted to Sullivan than he was to Wright. This attraction probably had something to do with the fact he was an exact contemporary of Sullivan and that his style was already well formed when he came into contact with the new American modernism. As Reyner Banham and H. L. C. Jaffé have shown, Wright meant more to the younger generation of Dutch architects, particularly to Oud, Rietveld, and Robert Van't Hoff.

In conclusion, something should be said about the parallel effects of Sullivan and Berlage on architecture in their respective countries. The essentially moral nature of Sullivan's approach to his work is well known; all his life he crusaded against sham and fakery in architecture, and even though he was defeated, he never gave up the fight. In much the same way, but perhaps with less flamboyance, Hendrik Berlage also fought for honesty in building. Sigfried Giedion in

Space, Time, and Architecture quite properly considers Berlage in a section entitled "The Demand for Morality in Architecture"; and no less a figure than Mies van der Rohe stated that his great design for the Library and Administration Building at Illinois Institute of Technology would never have been achieved without the stimulus of Berlage's untiring quest for structural integrity.

Small wonder then that, according to his family and friends, Berlage always felt a deep sense of kinship with Sullivan. They stood for many of the same principles.

Notes

1. The information in these paragraphs is contained in a letter from William Gray Purcell to the writer, 1 March 1956. This and other Purcell material has been deposited in the library of the College of Architecture and Design, Ann Arbor, Michigan.

2. *The Boston Evening Transcript,* December 9, 1911, p. 6.

3. In "American Influences on Late Nineteenth Century Architecture in the Netherlands," *Journal of the Society of Architectural Historians* 29 (1970): 163–174, the Dutch art historian A. W. Reinink brilliantly analyzes the Richardsonian elements in the Bourse. He concludes, however, that it was really a very eclectic building.

4. Berlage's articles, "Neuere amerikanische Architektur," are conveniently available in English translation in *The Literature of Architecture,* ed. Don Gifford (New York, 1966), pp. 606–616.

In order to evaluate the impact of American architecture on
the European architectural world of 1890–1914, it will be
useful to review the careers of the men discussed in this
book. Their lives have many striking parallels as well as a
number of significant differences. The oldest is Charles
Harrison Townsend, who was born in 1852. The youngest
is Eliel Saarinen, born in 1873. All of them therefore matured
in the 1880s and 1890s when Richardson and Sullivan were
at the height of their creative powers. In these decades their
work was being extensively published in the United States
and abroad. The bibliography of European writings on Richardson which appears on pages 333–334 of Henry-Russell
Hitchcock's *The Architecture of H. H. Richardson and His
Times,* rev. ed. (Cambridge, Massachusetts, 1966) is impressive. To this list it is, in effect, necessary to add the important
work of Graef and Hinckeldeyn, *Neubauten in Nordamerika*
(Berlin, 1897 and 1905). As I have attempted to show, it was
probably even more important than the periodical literature
on Richardson.

Unfortunately no bibliography of European writings on Sullivan has yet been compiled. We know, however, that André
Bouilhet, a Commissioner of the Union centrale des arts
décoratifs, was so impressed with the Transportation
Building at the 1893 World's Fair that he asked Sullivan
for material for the Musée des arts décoratifs in Paris. Sullivan donated a model of the Golden Door of the Transportation Building and casts of the doors of the Wainwright
Tomb and the Getty Tomb. Hugh Morrison remarked that

this material was assembled in a special Sullivan section
of the museum, and after its exhibition created so much
interest that the directors of an art gallery in Moscow asked
to have duplicates made of the things on display. Subsequently so many other requests of a similar nature came in
that the museum granted special permission to a firm in
Paris to make replicas for various institutions throughout
Europe. In 1894 the Union Centrale des Arts Décoratifs
awarded Sullivan three medals in gold, silver, and bronze
for the Transportation Building.[1]

In addition to this exhibition there were appreciative articles in the American architectural press by such men as
Montgomery Schuyler, Russell Sturgis, and Robert Craik
McLean; these were certainly important in Glasgow. While
no substantial publications on Sullivan in German have as
yet been found, a Dane, Alfred Ravad, wrote a significant
article on him which probably affected Anton Rosen. William
Gray Purcell remembered that Hendrik Berlage was well
informed on Sullivan at the time of their meeting in 1906.
In short, there was plenty of material available for any European architect who was interested in either Richardson or
Sullivan.

Several of the architects studied were able to travel in the
United States. Ferdinand Boberg actually worked in the office of Adler and Sullivan. Adolf Loos never worked in any
American architectural office but absorbed a good deal
nonetheless. "Burnet," says Andor Gomme, "must have spent
much of his time in America studying the new steel-framed
structures,"[2] and he notes particularly the influence of the
Wainwright Building in St. Louis on the Scotchman's work.
Charles Herbert Reilly made no less than six trips across the
Atlantic and possibly had a larger acquaintance in the American architectural profession than any of the others. He,
however, was the only one for whom the neoclassicism of
McKim, Mead & White had any great appeal. Undoubtedly
the most important single journey was that of Berlage. His
publications and lectures on American architecture coin-
cided in time very closely with the great German publications
of the work of Frank Lloyd Wright. He himself was closer to
Sullivan in the actual design of his buildings.

Aside from their American trips, these men were cosmo-
politan personalities who traveled widely on the Continent
and often spoke languages other than their own. Karl Moser
traveled in Italy and Greece, and Charles Harrison Townsend
also knew the Continent well. Eliel Saarinen spent a good
deal of time in Germany in connection with commissions

there and went to Vienna to study the work of Otto Wagner and the Sezession architects. In the twenties Adolf Loos was perhaps more at home in Paris and on the French Riviera than he was in his native Austria, though he never learned to speak the language, probably because of his deafness. For these men America was a significant part of the architectural world. Perhaps the most provincial of the lot was Lars Sonck, who apparently never traveled outside Scandinavia.

With a few exceptions these architects took a moralistic view of the problem of architectural design. They believed that most of what was being done around them was false, and, with the exception of Burnet and Reilly, they were convinced that a revival of the historic styles was out of the question. The architecture of the past was inadequate to the needs of the present. Berlage's insistence on structural honesty is well known. Saarinen told his biographer that the architecture that he knew in his youth was all sham and fakery. Moser is remembered for his courageous part in the League of Nations jury of 1927. Burnet, who was one of the most gifted designers in the group, adhered to the nineteenth-century tradition of using a polished neoclassical manner in monumental public buildings and what was almost an English version of the Chicago School in his commercial work. He repeats the approach of Schinkel. On the whole, however, they seem to have been attracted to Richardson and Sullivan by the ruggedness and honesty of their work. In Hinckeldeyn's writings the word *Sachlichkeit* was used many times, long before it came into popularity in the 1920s.

At this point an evaluation of the response of these architects to the new American forms is appropriate. Much has been written by students of American civilization on the mysterious transmutation that ideas undergo when they cross the Atlantic from east to west. Here we have the opposite case. Was there anything characteristically European in the handling of the novel forms of Richardson and Sullivan? The question is best answered in terms of national tradition. Except for the steeply pitched roof, which is thoroughly Germanic, it would be difficult to differentiate between Karl Moser's parish house for the Lutherkirche at Karlsruhe and comparable structures in the United States. Similarly the Göteborg libraries can be profitably compared with the Detroit Y.M.C.A. of 1890 by Mason and Rice. On the basis of form alone it would be hard to say which was in Michigan and which was in Sweden.

On the other hand, there is something extremely Viennese in Adolf Loos's treatment of Richardsonian motifs in the interiors done in the early years of his practice. The spatial design, the proportions, and the scale are much more constricted than in the American examples that he used as models. In the same way the Finnish Richardsonian of Saarinen and Sonck can be told at a glance from the work of Peabody and Stearns or Shepley, Rutan and Coolidge. The reason for this ease of discrimination is undoubtedly to be found in the fact that these architects were trying very hard, and with considerable success, to be Finnish. The cultural situation pushed them in this direction. Among all the Richardsonian architects in Europe, Sonck was probably the strongest designer. He seems to have had a very deep feeling for the manner of the American master.

All of these architects had long careers, and some of them accomplished their best work well after the period with which this book is concerned. It is doubtful if Loos ever did anything finer than his Muller house in 1930 in Prague. Sonck's Helsinki warehouses of the 1920s are equally impressive. Eliel Saarinen, the youngest of the group, enjoyed a kind of late flowering after he came to the United States. His Kingswood Girls' School of 1934–1936 at Bloomfield Hills, Michigan, is among his very best buildings. Ferdinand Boberg, on the other hand, declined in creative vigor after the turn of the century. In his later years he was not really a force to be reckoned with in Swedish architecture. More than the others he experienced the cultural isolation of

Mackintosh and, for that matter, of Sullivan. In any case, it is important to recognize that the later work of this generation bore little or no relation to the earlier or American phase. Loos, for example, was powerfully affected by the international style of the 1920s, and Saarinen was influenced by Wright. Among the late works considered in this book, Berlage's Christian Science church of 1924 and Burnet's Adelaide House of 1921–1924 would have to be considered exceptions to this generalization in the degree of their Americanism.

To a remarkable extent these architects were active in the provincial centers of European civilization rather than in the great capitals. Curjel and Moser built mostly in Mannheim and Karlsruhe, although some important work is located in Basel and Zurich. Saarinen's Richardsonian buildings are generally in Helsinki, and the largest surviving number of Swedish Richardsonian structures is in Göteborg. Here again Burnet, who was the most successful of the group in terms of the volume of his practice, is the exception. He operated offices in both Glasgow and London, and his American buildings can be seen in both cities. One is impressed, however, with the greater vitality of the Glasgow examples.[3] It would appear that Richardson and Sullivan had an appeal for architects working on the periphery of European culture rather than in the traditional centers. One looks in vain for American architecture in Paris, Rome, and Berlin. Vienna is a somewhat different case. There is no doubt that the architects of that city were aware of American work, but their own movement, the Sezession, was so strong and so well led that, with the exception of Loos's early apartment remodelings, they felt no need to develop the ideas of Richardson and Sullivan. There is, however, more than enough American-inspired work visible in Great Britain and on the Continent to allow us to state that Richardson and Sullivan, not Wright, were the first American architects of worldwide importance.

All of which brings us to the curious historiography of the problem. Why did historians of the Modern Movement overlook this significant body of material until the late 1950s? The answer is to be sought in the beliefs of the men who wrote histories of modern architecture in the twenties and thirties. For the most part these were individuals who were strong partisans of the international style and were deeply enmeshed in the ideology of the Bauhaus. Perhaps the most influential were Henry-Russell Hitchcock, Walter Curt Behrendt, and Sigfried Giedion. While their views of the development of modern architecture differed in many ways, they all stressed the key role played by Wright in relation to the De Stijl movement in the Nethlerlands and to the important German work of the 1920s. Hence they tended to overlook the possible connections between Richardson and Sullivan and the generation that Hitchcock called "the New Traditionalists" in his *Modern Architecture: Romanticism and Reintegration* of 1929. This was perhaps an understandable error. Wright was, after all, an overwhelming figure, and there was an obvious relationship between a building like the Robie house of 1908–1909 and the Barcelona Pavilion of Mies van der Rohe in 1929. It was hard to believe that any American architect of the late nineteenth century could have had a similar impact in Europe. Thus Giedion simply ignored the international aspects of Richardson and Sullivan in the first edition of his *Space, Time, and Architecture* (Cambridge, Massachusetts, 1941), and Behrendt, a Nazi refugee who had himself been active in the great housing programs of the Weimar Republic, could write, "Without being guilty of exaggeration, one may justly assert that Frank Lloyd Wright's work is the first creation in the realm of architecture that can be regarded as an independent contribution of the American spirit to European culture."[4] If we may return to the theme of the first chapter, it would appear that American literature has generally been more fortunate in its historiography. Whitman and Emerson were considered as world figures in their own lifetimes, although it is interesting to note that we have had to wait until the middle of this century for really thoughtful appraisals of their international impact.

Another feature of the problem is, of course, that in the twenties and thirties the necessary spadework on the early careers of the "New Traditionalists" had not been done. It was therefore not at all clear that this generation of architects was in any way affected by American work. Still, Giedion, for example, must have known Karl Moser more or less well, and it is hard to believe that they did not discuss Richardson together. It is pleasant to note that Hitchcock has made magnificent amends for his earlier omission. No scholar has taken a more international view of the development of modern architecture. The conclusion, however, is inescapable. Historians have hitherto underestimated the European role of America in architecture during the crucial decades 1890–1910. It is now time to rectify this error.

Notes

1. Hugh Morrison, *Louis Sullivan: Prophet of Modern Architecture* (New York, 1962), p. 189.

2. Andor Gomme and David Walker, *Architecture of Glasgow* (London, 1968), p. 205.

3. Final judgments on Burnet will have to be suspended until the appearance of the book that Professor Gomme and Mr. Walker have in preparation.

4. Walter Curt Behrendt, *Modern Building: Its Nature, Problems, and Forms* (New York, 1937), p. 139.

A Note on
Bibliography

For the most part the literary sources of this work are given in the footnotes. There are, however, a few other works on the period that should be mentioned. Even though I have disagreed with it sharply, Sigfried Giedion's *Space, Time, and Architecture,* 5th ed., rev. and enl. (Cambridge, Mass., 1967), remains an important work and must be consulted by all students of the Modern Movement. Reyner Banham's *Theory and Design in the First Machine Age* (London, 1960) is a useful corrective to Giedion and is particularly good in its treatment of Wright's impact on Dutch architects. Bruno Zevi's *Storia dell' architettura moderna* (Turin, 1953) is also excellent. An English translation is much needed.

On the general relations of European and American culture in the late nineteenth century, no book is more rewarding than Leon Edel's magistral biography of Henry James. Four volumes have thus far appeared: *Henry James: The Untried Years* (Philadelphia and New York, 1953), *Henry James: The Conquest of London* (Philadelphia and New York, 1962), *Henry James: The Middle Years* (Philadelphia and New York, 1962), and *Henry James: The Treacherous Years* (Philadelphia and New York, 1969). We await the last.

There is, of course, an enormous literature on the history of American painting, but not many scholars see it as a part of the culture of the Western world. One of the few who make this attempt is E. P. Richardson in his old but still rewarding *The Way of Western Art* (Cambridge, Massachusetts, 1939). Such excellent works as Milton Brown, *American Painting from the Armory Show to the Great Depression* (Princeton, 1955), are primarily concerned with the impact of European art on American painters. Among books on abstract expressionism, Irving Sandler, *The Triumph of American Painting* (New York, 1970), has some provocative pages on the Franco-American interaction, and Maurice Tuchman, *New York School: The First Generation* (New York, 1965), reprints many excellent statements by artists and critics.

Serious books on British architecture in the Edwardian age

are curiously lacking. For domestic work the three volumes of Hermann Muthesius on *Das englische Haus* (Berlin, 1908) are still fundamental. Charles H. Reilly wrote an interesting autobiography, *Scaffolding in the Sky* (London, 1938), but there is very little material on the great stylists such as Burnet and Blomfield. A provocative article by David Gebhard, "C. F. A. Voysey — To and From America," appears in vol. 30 (1971), pp. 304–312 of the *Journal of the Society of Architectural Historians.* It deals with the possible impact on Voysey of American architecture in the 1880s. The situation in Germany and Austria is somewhat better, though the connections of Berlin and Vienna with the United States have still not been fully explained. The firm of Curjel and Moser had the useful habit of publishing illustrated accounts of each of its church building projects. A collection of these pamphlets is available in the library of the Eidgenossische Technische Hochschule in Zurich, and I relied on it heavily. Their work was also published in most of the leading architectural periodicals of the time.

Any study of Adolf Loos must begin with his own *Sämtliche Schriften* (Vienna and Munich, 1962). The appendix is useful but could be amplified for American readers. Among secondary works Ludwig Münz and Gustav Künstler, *Adolf Loos: Pioneer of Modern Architecture,* trans. Harold Meek (New York and Washington, 1966), is noteworthy, though the text is disorganized and shows an excessively adulatory attitude. It may be supplemented by the older work of Loos's pupil, Heinrich Kulka, *Adolf Loos: Das Werk des Architekten* (Vienna, 1931). Mention should also be made of the remarkable exhibition catalogue of Otto Antonia Graf, *Die vergessene Wagnerschule* (Vienna, Museum of the Twentieth Century, 1969). Some of the projects are extremely Wrightian in feeling. For the general atmosphere of pre–World War I Vienna, Stefan Zweig, *The World of Yesterday* (New York, 1943), is excellent.

On the Scandinavian scene the key article is Kay Fisker,

"Internationalism contra Nationalromantik," in *Arkitekten*
22 (1960): 369–387. Fisker also wrote an obituary of Anton
Rosen for *Arkitekten* 30 (1928): 157–158. For Boberg and
Clason the references cited in the text are generally sufficient. I have been informed that Professor Harald Wideen
of the City Historical Museum in Göteborg is at work on a
study of Hans Hedlund.

For Eliel Saarinen the best available work is the biography
by Albert Christ-Janer, *Eliel Saarinen* (Chicago, 1948), with
a foreword by Alvar Aalto. Its treatment of his Finnish phase
is, however, insufficient. The best consideration of Finnish
work in the early twentieth century is the section entitled
"Towards Modern Architecture" in Nils Erick Wickberg, *Finnish Architecture* (Helsinki, 1962). Unhappily, there is as yet
no book on Lars Sonck. An old but still valuable survey of the
period is *Finsk Arkitektur* (Helsinki, 1904); the photographs
are remarkable. Two recent critics have noticed the Richardsonian flavor in this work. They are J. M. Richards, *A Guide
to Finnish Architecture* (London, 1966), and Henry-Russell
Hitchcock, "Aalto versus Aalto: The Other Finland," *Perspecta,* nos. 9–10 (1965), pp. 132–166.

On Hendrik Berlage, one of the truly outstanding figures of
the Modern Movement, no comprehensive book as yet exists.
The standard work is Jan Gratama, *Dr. H. P. Berlage, Bouw-
meester* (Rotterdam, 1925), but it pays no attention to the
impact of his American journey. It is good to know that a new
work on Berlage is in prospect from Pieter Singelenberg of
the University of Utrecht.

Finally, there is the contribution of Henry-Russell Hitchcock on "American Influence Abroad" in *The Rise of an
American Architecture,* ed. Edgar Kaufmann, Jr. (New York,
1970). This essay is a brilliant summary of all the work that
has been done on the subject to date. The present volume is
in certain respects an amplification of suggestions contained
therein.

Henry-Russell Hitchcock, *The Architecture of H. H. Richardson and His Times* (Cambridge: M.I.T. Press, 1966)
35

A. F. Kersting
3

Lichtbildwerkstätte "Alpenland," Vienna
67, 68

Museum für Angewandte Kunst, Vienna
5, 6, 7, 33, 34, 36, 37, 38, 39, 45, 47, 63, 69, 70, 72

Museum of the City of New York
130

Museum of the City of Vienna
62, 71

N. I. Associates (Gerald Mansheim)
136

Reginald Pound, *Selfridge* (London: William Heinemann, Ltd., 1960)
25

Preussische Staatsbibliothek, Berlin
54, 55

Progressive Architecture 37 (November, 1950), p. 138
128

Simo Rista
103

Douglas Scott
17

Asko Salokorpi
108, 109

Pieter Singelenberg
133

G. E. Kidder Smith, *Sweden Builds* (Reinhold Publishing Corporation, New York, 1957)
81

G. E. Kidder Smith, *Switzerland Builds* (A. Bonnier, New York, 1950)
31, 32

Teknisk Tidskrift
97, 98

Theodore Turak
56, 57

Mariana Van Rensselaer, *Henry Hobson Richardson and His Works* (Park Forest, Ill.: The Prairie School Press, 1967)
46, 64, 82